FROM THE BIRMINGHAM MUSEUM OF ART

CULINARY
MASTERPIECES

FROM THE BIRMINGHAM MUSEUM OF ART

PRESENTED BY THE VOLUNTEERS OF THE MUSEUM

CULINARY MASTERPIECES

(Cover) William Merritt Chase (American 1849–1916, *Still Life with Watermelon*, 1868. Oil on canvas, 28 x 24 inches. Gift in memory of Mrs. Margaret Woodward Evins Spencer, by her family.

William Merritt Chase painted this work, his first still life, when he was only twenty years old, revealing his enormous talent, even at this young age. His formal training up to this time had been only modest instruction from two local Indianapolis artists. But it is clear from the quality of this work that he was an artist whose further training and work would number him among America's best.
The strong use of light and shadow, the rich, vivid coloring, and Chase's ability to render textures, such as those in the tablecloth, glass, polished wooden table top, and metal bowl, give this painting its special appeal to the viewer. We can almost taste and smell the sweet, juicy fruit.

(Frontispiece) Christophe Huet (died 1759), *La Boisson chaude (The Hot Drink)*, ca. 1750. Oil on canvas, 119 1/2 x 53 1/4 inches. Museum purchase with funds provided by the 1992 Museum Dinner and Ball and the Acquisitions Fund, Inc.

This detail is from one of four French wall panels that once graced an eighteenth-century French dining room. The depiction of picnic scenes inhabited with lavishly dressed Chinese figures, succulent food and drink, and exotic animals, suggests that these panels were part of a larger room decoration that may have included paintings on the ceiling, and over the mantel, windows, and doors. They were done at a time when a passion for all things Oriental pervaded the decorative arts of Europe. The panels, known as "arabesques", also contain a canopy at the top adorned with floral garlands and brightly colored ribbons, and, at the bottom, scenes of birds, monkeys in eighteenth-century costumes, and medallions painted *en grisailles* (in greys only).

Recipes from *The Delectable Past*
© 1964 Esther B. Aresty

To order additional copies, please use the order form at the back of this book.

ISBN 0-931394-34-1

This cookbook was designed by Joan Kennedy, with cover and lead-in pages designed by Kendra Lambert.
Color photography was by Robert Linthout, Harold Kilgore, and Owen Murphy.
Photo on page 11 courtesty *Southern Accents*, photographed by Mick Hale.
It was typeset in Kabel Book and output by Compos-It, Inc., Montgomery, Alabama.
Color separations by Precision Color, Inc., Birmingham, Alabama.
It was printed on Frostbrite 80 lb. text by EBSCO Media, Inc., Birmingham, Alabama.

CONTENTS

Cookbook Committee of the Volunteers of the Birmingham Museum of Art

Helen Bryant Smith
Chairman
Dorothy H. Barton
Ida Martha Dimick
Susan Johnston
Joan Menendez
Co-Chairmen

Food Editors
Bette Blumenthal
Gerda Carmichael
Lell Conner
Jane Graham
Ethel Howard
Chris Kirkland
Suzanne Lucas
Jane Menendez
Susan Rouse
Babbie Shelton
Sara Sistrunk
Marilyn Smith
Jonnie Venglik
Cynthia Willingham

Marketing
Marcia Cohen
Chairman
Pat Weil
Co-Chairman
Dot Barton
Bette Blumenthal
Lell Conner
June Emory
Bobbie Howell
Phoebe Howell
Susan Johnston
Joan Menendez
Susan Moore
Susan Rouse
Sara Sistrunk
Helen B. Smith
Jim Stapleton

Finance
Helen B. Smith
Chairman
Ida Martha Dimick
Susan Rouse
Helen McMaster

Art
Esta Kamplain
Chairman
Evelyn Allen
Susan Johnston
Pat Millhouse
Sara Sistrunk
Helen B. Smith

6

We wish to thank the following restaurants who contributed to this cookbook

Anthony's
The Back Alley
Benedikt's
Blue & White Café
Bombay Café
Bottega Restaurant
   and Café
The Bright Star
Buttiker's Café

Cabana Café
C'est Bon
Christian's
Continental Bakery
Cosmo's Pizza
Dexter's on Hollywood
Fox Valley
Highlands Bar and Grill
Joe Bar

Kathy G's Catering
Klingler's European Bakery
La Paz
Meadowlark Farm
Sheraton Civic Center
   Atrium Restaurant
Tutwiler Hotel
Vincent's Market
Zelda's

ACKNOWLEDGMENTS

This cookbook was compiled from recipes submitted by members of the Birmingham Museum of Art, its volunteers, staff, and curators. Those who submitted recipes do not claim that all are original, only that they are treasured favorites of family and friends. We thank them first, for without their recipes there would be no book.

A committee from the Volunteer Council had the happy pleasure of cooking, tasting, and coming together in a spirit of comraderie to evaluate during 1991 and 1992. The Cookbook Committee met and carefully tested each recipe and in some instances made minor changes in order to update or enhance its presentation. Space constraints and similarity of content prevented us from including all the recipes submitted; however, the recipes included are a delightful mix of old, new, classic, and light, and are incredibly delicious. We hope this collection will have a broad appeal for those who love to cook and entertain, as well as inspire new homemakers.

With the help of the musuem's directors and curators, a committee from the Volunteer Council, made up mostly of docents who know the collection well, chose the art reproduced herein.

This book would not have been possible without the contributions, help, and advice of a number of people. We would like to thank the Birmingham restaurants who submitted some of their best recipes; to Martha Johnston of *Southern Living*, whose long experience in this field made her advice invaluable; to Jennifer Greer for her expertise in copy editing; and to EBSCO Media, whose cooperation, advice, and expertise have helped to make this book so visually appealing. We would also like to add a special thanks to Esther B. Aresty for allowing us to use recipes from her delightful book, *The Delectabel Past*. And to *Southern Accents* and photograher Mick Hale for the use of the photograph of the New York apartment of Eugenia Woodward Hitt.

The Birmingham Museum of Art owes a debt of gratitude to the special people without whose hard work and dedication this cookbook would not have been possible: to Chamsie Phillips for conceiving the idea and getting it off the ground; to Helen Smith for taking over as chairman of the Cookbook Committee and putting in untold hours of work in organization, meetings, and testing, always with a gracious smile and friendly demeanor; to Gail Trechsel who, as acting director of the museum during most of the duration of the work, never waivered in her support and encouragement; to the Volunteer Cookbook Committee whose total commitment in time, money, organizing, testing, and research, we will never be able to repay; and finally, to Joan Kennedy, who carried the heaviest load of all. Her enthusiasm, creativity, multi-talents, and devotion to the project inspired the committee more than she will ever know.

Contributors and Testers

We thank all of those, their families and friends, who contributed and/or tested the recipes. They have given generously of their time and talents to assure quality and excellence.

Bryding Adams
Tracey Albainy
Margaret Alexander
Harry Andress
Donna Antoon
Marsha Asman
Frances R. Bailey
Sara Jane Ball
Peggy Balliet
Lula Barnett
Dorothy Barton
James C. Barton
JuJu Beale
Fred A. Beam
Jean Bearman
Terry Beckham
Nancy Bennett
Mrs. A. C. L. Bernard
Mrs. James S. Best
Joice Benedikt
Anne Blair
Mrs. J. C. Blakey
Bette Blumenthal
Helen Bolvig
Mary Gene Boulware
Mrs. John H. Brewer
Leigh Bromberg
Mrs. Percy Brower
Evelyn C. Brown
Ruth Alys Brown
Ann Bruno
Grace Burleigh
Cynthia Butler
Catherine Cabaniss
Eivor H. Callahan
Gerda Carmichael
Bobbie Carnwath
Jan K. Cash
Daphne Chamberlin
Barbara D. Chenoweth
Mrs. A. I. Chenoweth

Billie Cheyney
Barbara Childs
Eloise Clark
Gail Clark
Una Coleman
Tippy Coley
Donald Comer
Mrs. Donald Comer III
Lell Conner
Rebecca Cooper
Carolyn Crawmer
Paula Crockard
Anne Crow
Frances B. Crowder
Sara Crowder
Mrs. Gene M. Cushman
Elizabeth Daniel
Margaret Dauber
Jacqui David
Mrs. Guerry M. Denson
Faye Tynes Dick
Ida Martha Dimick
Rae Earley
Ellen Elsas
Lee Elsas
Carolyn Emmons
Ruth S. Engel
Beverly B. Erdreich
Katherine Estes
Barb Exum
Mrs. Theodore W. Fendley
Marcia Finkelstein
Pearl Gantt
Andrea Simpson Garrett
Jeanne Gentle
John and Jill Gemmill
Jane Graham
Ethel Griffin
Betty Grisham
Liz Haberstock
Carol L. Hall

Cathy Harvey
Leah Boston Hathcock
Jan Henger
Carson Herrington
Elizabeth Hester
Renae Hewitt
Mrs. W. Price Hightower, Jr.
Margaret Anderson Hipp
Mary Louise Hodges
Jackie Hoffman
Ethel Howard
Bobbie Howell
Jim and Sue Huffer
Tita Hyland
Sheryl Isobe
Gloria Israel
Pat Jehle
Sally W. Johnson
Susan Johnston
Wende Johnston
Esta Kamplain
Vicki Jo Kemp
Joan K. Kennedy
Jennifer Kimbrell
Frances H. Kimbrough
Carolyn King
Chris Kirkland
Thomas Kirkland
Barbara Lanier
Fred LeJeune
Jean Liles
Margaret Livingston
Suzanne Lucas
Michelle Luria
Nancy B. McCormack
Carol McCoy
Karen McElroy
Regina McFadden
Helen McMaster
Louise McSpadden
Kristin Manthey

Jane Menendez
Joan Menendez
Pat Millhouse
Robert Moffett
Nancy Morrow
Dee Morgan
Ellen Mosley
Mrs. James R. Nelson
Pauline M. Neville
Myra Odess
Mrs. Burton D. Olshan
Mrs. Guy H. Orr
Susan Orr
Shirley Palmes
Cora S. Paris
Ailene Parnell
Sara S. Perry
Diane Presley Pettus
Carol Petty
Martha Pharo
Chamsie Phillips
Margie Poole
Sarah S. Porter
Sheldon Reid
Betty Renneker
Louise S. Rice
Wendell Riggins
Cindy Riley
Susan Rouse
Gailya Graves Sargent
Elizabeth Secor
Rena Selfe
Mary Lou Shaw
Babbie Shelton
Mrs. Richard B. Shepard
Frances Shepherd
Dorothy B. Shiland
Mrs. Pascal Shook
Sara Sistrunk
Nan Skier
Mrs. E. Hartwell K. Smith
Helen B. Smith
Marilyn Smith
Edna Snow
Helen Snow

Frances C. Sommers
William M. Spencer III
Jane Sparkes
Valora H. Spencer
Trudy Wilner Stack
John Stadtlander
Mrs. Bernard Steiner
Mary Catherine Stringfellow
Barbara Sturgeon
Cacky Sullivan
Julia Thomason
Mary John Tiller
Jonnie Venglik
Mary Villadsen
Jane Darnell Walker
Edith Wallace
Mrs. John B. Walters
Kenny Walters
Nancy Warren
Dorothy Watters
Patricia Weaver
Pat Weil
Wilma Whitaker
Frances W. Wideman
Lorene P. Williams
Shannon Williams
Cynthia Willingham
Donald A. Wood
Polly Wood

10

INTRODUCTION

(Page 9) Dining Room in the former apartment of Eugenia Woodward Hitt, 720 Park Avenue, New York (photographed in 1991) (objects now in the permanent collection of the Birmingham Museum of Art).

Birmingham native Eugenia Woodward Hitt bequeathed the contents of her New York apartment to the Birmingham Museum of Art in 1990. The two thousand objects, paintings, and drawings in this important collection include canvases by the French painters Fragonard, Pater, Lancret, and Tocqué, among others, and more than thirty Meissen porcelain figures of birds, English furniture and silver, and an exhaustive assemblage of eighteenth-century French furniture, clocks, silver, and gilt bronze wall lights and firedogs. In this photograph, the English Regency dining table is set with an early nineteenth-century English pearlware service, Sheffield candlesticks, and a silver tureen made in Paris around 1780.

James Abbott McNeill Whistler (American, 1834–1903), *The Kitchen*, 1858. Etching with drypoint, 8 15/16 x 6 1/8 inches. Bequest of Mr. and Mrs. Oscar Wells.

James McNeill Whistler, considered one of the great American artists of the nineteenth century, actually spent the majority of his life in Europe. As a young artist, Whistler journeyed down the Rhine with sketch pad and etching plates in his knapsack, recording his journey in a series of romantic farm scenes, interiors, and portraits. From this body of work, Whistler published his first set of prints, *The Twelve Etchings from Nature*, also known as *The French Set. Kitchen Interior* comes from this series.

In this print, Whistler chose as subject matter the humble kitchen setting, using lighting to create a frame within a frame as the darkness of the interior contrasts with the natural light streaming through the window. The influence of Northern artists like Vermeer and Rembrandt is evident, yet Whistler's own style emerges in his use of fluid lines and his interest in atmospheric effects.

The history of the Birmingham Museum of Art is closley tied to volunteers and collectors in the community who had the vision and desire to establish an art museum for the benefit of the public. From 1908, with the founding of the Birmingham Art Club, to the opening of the galleries in City Hall in 1951, the spirit behind this dream did not falter. These efforts were followed by a bequest from a Birmingham citizen, Oscar Wells, which allowed the museum to build its own facility that opened in 1959. The Board of Trustees wanted the museum to be encyclopedic with important works from all periods, representing the breadth and diversity of aesthetic expression. Early gifts reflected this mission and included American and European paintings, Chinese ceramics, textiles, old master prints, costumes, and, most notably, twenty-nine Italian Renaissance paintings from the Samuel H. Kress Foundation.

Other collections soon developed through gift purchase, including the Beeson Collection of Wedgwood, English and European silver and porcelain, the Simon Collection of Remington bronzes, and American paintings, Asian, pre-Columbian, and Native American art. The 1980s saw the collections expand in scope and included the development of the African and photography collections. In 1991 the museum added an important collection of French furniture, porcelain, silver, and paintings of the eighteenth century, a gift of Eugenia Woodward Hitt.

The relatively recent founding of the art museum, coupled with restraints imposed by the art market, has not allowed the museum to represent all areas of artistic expression, but areas of real strength, as cited above, exist, and the museum continues to develop those strengths. The collections offer an introduction to world art history rivaling that of any museum within the deep South and the museum serves, through its collections and exhibitions, as an important educational and cultural resource for the state and region.

In selecting the illusrtations for this cookbook, an attempt was made to represent the strengths and "stars" of the collection, as well as those objects which have a direct link with food. The selection committee was composed of museum docents and other volunteers who really use the collection, in tours with the public and research for the staff. This entire effort, the museum's first cookbook, could not have been possible without the inspiration and dedication of the volunteers.

Gail A. Trechsel

APPETIZERS & BEVERAGES

(Page 15) Four vessels, Peru, Lambayeque region, Batan Grande complex, Sican culture, ca. 850–1050. Gold and copper alloy. Museum purchase.

These pieces are from a burial site in the Lambayeque area of northern coastal Peru. During the Middle Sican period (850–1050), the art of metallurgy was developed to a level of unmatched sophistication. These vessels are composed of thinly hammered *tumbaga*, an alloy of gold and copper. Designs were raised by hammering and embossing over wooden forms.

The large numbers of gold-worked objects found in Sican burials raises doubts that they were all manufactured strictly for funerary use. They are obviously of a ceremonial and not a common utilitarian nature. These objects were probably used during rituals throughout life, and were considered as indications of status.

APPETIZERS

BEVERAGES

A TART TO PROVOKE COURAGE EITHER IN MAN OR WOMAN

Take a quart of good wine and boile therein two Burre rootes scraped cleane, two good quinces, and a potato roote well pared, and an ounce of Dates, and when all these are boiled verie tender, let them be drawne through a strainer wine and al, and then be put in the yolks of eight eggs, and the braines of three or fower cocke sparrowes, and straine them into the other, and a little rosewater, and seeth them all with sugar, cinamon and ginger, and cloves and mace, and put in a little sweet butter, and set it upon a chafing dish of coales between two platters, & so let it boile til it be something big.

HOT CRAB DIP WITH BRANDY

Makes 5 cups

1 pound lump crabmeat
1/2 cup chopped green onions
1 [8 ounce] package cream cheese
1 cup heavy cream
3 shallots, finely chopped
3 tablespoons fresh dill
1/2 cup grated Parmesan cheese
1 teaspoon salt
1 teaspoon cayenne pepper
1 tablespoon olive oil
6 tablespoons brandy

- Sauté shallots in olive oil slowly until translucent.
- Add brandy to deglaze pan.
- Reduce by 1/2 and add heavy cream. Reduce by 1/3 and remove from heat.
- Soften cream cheese and whisk into mixture until smooth.
- Stir in Parmesan cheese, fresh basil, and chives.
- Fold in crabmeat and season.

Dip with crackers or melba toast.

The first recipe we offer is one you might not rush to the kitchen to prepare. It is from *The Good Huswives Handmaid*, published in England in 1597, and comes to us courtesy of *The Delectable Past*. It is the first of a number of vintage recipes we have included in this cookbook. Some, like this, are for pure reading enjoyment, others are as delicious today as when the cookbooks were published. For these, we have provided contemporary measurements and ingredients.

This recipe comes to us courtesy of Vincent's Market. In the relatively short time Vincent's has been a part of Birmingham cuisine, it has gained the reputation of having superb meats, seafood, produce, baked goods, and a gourmet deli section surpassed by none. It is the place to go for ingredients available nowhere else in town, and also where you can find the delicious Hot Crab Dip with Brandy we include here.

17

This recipe was submitted by Tita Hyland, wife of the museum's former director, Douglas Hyland. She claims it is one of her best crowd pleasers.

⌒ HOT CRABMEAT SPREAD

Serves 15 to 20 (about 3 cups)

1 pound fresh crabmeat or 2 [6–ounce] cans crabmeat
2 [8–ounce] packages cream cheese, softened
1 cup sour cream
1/2 cup [2 ounces] grated Cheddar cheese
2 cloves garlic, minced
1 teaspoon dry mustard
2 tablespoons mayonnaise
2 tablespoons steak sauce
Juice of 1/2 lemon
1 [3– to 4–ounce] package slivered almonds

- Mix all ingredients together, except almonds.
- If the mixture is too dry, add milk to make it creamy.
- Lightly grease a 1 1/2–quart ovenproof casserole dish which can also be used for serving.
- Place mixture in pan.
- Top with almonds.
- Bake at 325° for 45 minutes.
- Serve with water crackers.

Good make-ahead dish

⌒ SALMON LOG

Serves 8 to 12

1 [16–ounce] can red salmon, drained and flaked, with skin and bones removed
1 [8–ounce] package cream cheese, softened
1 tablespoon lemon juice
2 tablespoons minced scallions
1 teaspoon horseradish
1 teaspoon liquid smoke (optional)
1/2 cup chopped walnuts or pecans
3 tablespoons finely chopped parsley

- Combine salmon with the next 5 ingredients and mix well. Chill for several hours.
- Combine nuts and parsley.
- Shape salmon mixture into a 8 x 2–inch log. Roll it in nut mixture. Chill well.

Serve with crackers

◥ SALMON MOUSSE

Makes about 3 cups

1 envelope unflavored gelatin
2 tablespoons cold water
1/2 teaspoon salt
1 tablespoon sugar
1 1/2 tablespoons all-purpose flour
2 teaspoons dry mustard
Large dash of cayenne pepper
2 egg yolks
3/4 cup milk
1/4 cup vinegar
1 1/2 tablespoons butter or margarine
1 [15 1/2–ounce] can red salmon, drained with skin and bones removed

- Dissolve gelatin in cold water. Set aside.
- In the top of a double boiler, mix remaining ingredients together except salmon; cook, stirring, until the mixture is thickened to a thin cream sauce.
- Remove from heat. Add gelatin.
- Add salmon, and stir till blended.
- Pour into a greased 3–cup mold.
- When chilled, unmold and, if desired, frost with mayonnaise.
- Serve with saltine crackers.

19

This recipe is for a mock crab dip and was submitted by Pat Jehle, who says it always fools the crowd. It is a convenient company dish since you usually have the ingredients on hand.

 POOR MAN'S CRAB SPREAD

Makes 1 1/2 cups

1 [3–ounce] package cream cheese, softened
2 teaspoons fresh lemon juice
2/3 cup sour cream
1 [0.6–ounce] package Italian salad dressing mix
1 [6 1/2–ounce] can water-packed white tuna, drained

• Mix cream cheese, lemon juice, sour cream, and Italian dressing together.
• Add tuna and blend it in with a fork.
• Serve chilled with crackers or raw vegetables.

Good make-ahead dish.

 MUSHROOM–CHICKEN LIVER PATÉ

Makes 2 cups

1/2 cup butter or margarine
1/2 pound fresh mushrooms
1 pound chicken livers
1 teaspoon garlic salt
1 teaspoon paprika
1/3 cup chopped spring onions
1/2 cup dry white wine
3 drops hot sauce
Salt to taste

• Sauté mushrooms, liver, garlic salt, paprika, and onions in 1/4 cup butter for 5 minutes.
• Add wine and hot sauce; cover and cook slowly for 5 to 10 minutes. Cool.
• Blend mixture in the blender, and add remaining butter and salt to taste.
• Turn into a 9–inch pie or quiche dish.
• Chill overnight.
• Decorate in concentric circles with red caviar, chopped olives, minced hard-boiled eggs.
• Serve with water crackers.

∾ HOT BEEF DIP

Makes 2 1/2 cups

1 [8–ounce] package cream cheese
1 [8–ounce] package lowfat sour cream
1 [2–ounce] jar dehydrated beef
2 tablespoons finely chopped green pepper
2 tablespoons finely chopped onion
1/2 cup finely chopped walnuts

- Combine cream cheese and sour cream mixing well; add beef, green pepper, and onion and stir to blend .
- Place mixture in small ovenproof casserole and bake at 350° for 15 minutes.
- Remove from oven and add walnuts.
- Serve hot with sturdy crackers.

∾ ISLAND TERIYAKI

Serves 12 to 16 as an appetizer

1/2 cup soy sauce
1/4 cup brown sugar
2 tablespoons olive oil
1 tablespoon grated ginger root or 1 teaspoon dry ginger
1/4 teaspoon cracked ground pepper
2 cloves fresh minced garlic
1 1/2 pounds top sirloin steak, cut in 1/4–inch by 1–inch wide strips
1 [8–ounce] can whole water chestnuts

- In a deep bowl, combine all ingredients except steak and water chestnuts. Mix well.
- Add meat strips and stir to coat.
- Marinate 4 hours in the refrigerator.
- Lace meat accordion-style on skewers, placing a water chestnut at each end of the meat. (Thin metal skewers are best, to keep the water chestnuts from breaking.)
- Grill over hot coals or broil 4 to 6 inches from broiler flame for 10 to 12 minutes. Turn frequently and baste with marinade while cooking.

This recipe is for the national dish of what used to be Yugoslavia. To the children who live in the region, it is like hamburgers to American kids. No matter what happens politically in this area, the dish will remain a favorite. The recipe varies from region to region, made of various combinations of lamb, pork, and beef, but is delicious no matter which you use.

∾ CEVAPCICI

Serves 12 to 20 as an appetizer, 4 to 6 as an entrée

1 tablespoon margarine or butter
1/2 cup finely chopped onion
1/2 teaspoon finely chopped garlic
1 pound ground beef chuck
1 pound ground pork or lamb
1 egg white, lightly beaten
1 teaspoon salt
1/2 teaspoon pepper
1 to 1 1/2 tablespoons Hungarian paprika
Finely chopped onion
Chili sauce or tiny hot peppers

- Sauté onion and garlic in melted butter until onion is lightly browned.
- Place in a large bowl; add meat, egg white, salt, pepper, and paprika. Mix together well.
- Shape meat mixture into cylinders that are approximately 3/4 inch wide and 2 inches long.
- Place the cylinders on a plate, cover with wax paper, and chill at least 1 hour until meat is firm.
- Arrange on metal skewers, running through the sides, not the ends, and leaving at least 1/4 inch between cylinders.
- Grill on a hot grill or broil 4 to 6 inches from the broiler flame, about 8 minutes on each side, or until they are dark brown on the outside and well done on the inside. They may also be fried in a heavy skillet, turning often.
- Serve with finely chopped onion and chili sauce or tiny hot peppers.

A combination of the three ground meats may be used, using varying amounts of all, or just one.

❧ CHEESE RING WITH STRAWBERRY JAM

Makes 3 1/2 to 4 cups

4 cups [16 ounces] grated sharp Cheddar cheese
1 cup chopped pecans
3/4 cup mayonnaise
1 medium onion, grated
1 clove garlic, pressed
1/2 teaspoon hot sauce
1 cup strawberry jam

- Mix all ingredients together, except strawberry jam.
- Form into a ring on a serving plate.
- Put strawberry jam in center of ring.

Serve with crackers.

❧ LONDON CHEESE LOG

Makes 4 3/4 cups

11 ounces cream cheese, softened
4 ounces bleu cheese, softened
1 cup thinly sliced ripe olives
2 cups coarsely chopped walnuts or pecans

- Blend cheeses thoroughly in a large bowl with an electric mixer. Stir in olives and 1 cup of nuts.
- Spread remaining nuts on a sheet of wax paper.
- Flour hands and shape cheese mixture into 1 long or 2 short logs. (For easier handling, chill the cheese mixture until firm.) Roll log in nuts until it is well coated.
- Wrap in wax paper and refrigerate overnight.
- Serve with crackers or melba toast.

Good make-ahead dish.
Freezes well.

This appetizer recipe, submitted by Helen Snow, came with a warning not to serve it with a large spoon because people are apt to eat it as a dessert rather than an appetizer.

❧ HAWAIIAN CHEESE BALL

Makes 3 1/2 cups

2 [8–ounce] packages cream cheese, softened
1 [8 1/2–ounce] can crushed pineapple, well drained
1/4 cup finely chopped green pepper
1 tablespoon grated onion
1 tablespoon seasoned salt
2 cups chopped pecans

- Mix all ingredients together, except 1 cup of pecans.
- Chill until firm.
- Form into a ball or loaf.
- Roll in remaining cup of pecans.
- Serve with assorted crackers.

 DILL DIP FOR CRUDITÉ

Makes 2 cups

2 cups lowfat sour cream
1 teaspoon horseradish
1 tablespoon paprika
1 tablespoon chopped chives
1 teaspoon salt
2 teaspoons dill weed
1/8 teaspoon pepper
1 clove garlic, crushed

• Mix all ingredients together and chill overnight.
• Serve with raw vegetables.

CRUDITÉ DIP

Makes 4 1/2 cups

2 cups mayonnaise
2 cups sour cream
3 tablespoons minced fresh parsley
3 tablespoons grated onion
3 tablespoons dried dill weed
1 1/2 tablespoons seasoned salt

• Blend all ingredients together.
• Chill and serve with raw vegetables.

Also good on baked potatoes

SUN-DRIED TOMATO DIP

Makes 2 cups

1 [8–ounce] package cream cheese, softened
12 to 15 sun-dried tomatoes, packed in oil, drained
   with1 tablespoon oil reserved
2 to 3 cloves garlic

• Place cream cheese, tomatoes, garlic, and 1 tablespoon oil in a food processor
  or blender and process until well-blended, but not creamy.
• Serve with raw vegetables, torilla chips, or seafood.

25

This recipe was submitted by Barbara Childs who claims if you try this just once, you will love it forever!

 **MEXICAN BEAN DIP**

Makes 3 cups

2 [10 1/2–ounce] cans ready to serve chili beef soup
1 [4–ounce] can chopped green chilies, mild or hot
1 [2 1/4–ounce] can sliced ripe olives
2 cups [8 ounces] grated Cheddar cheese
1/2 large onion, chopped

- Mix all the ingredients together in 1 1/2–quart ovenproof casserole dish that can be used for serving.
- Heat in oven at 350° for about 30 minutes, or until hot and gooey.
- Keep dip warm on a warming tray or in a serving dish with a heat source while serving.

Serve with corn chips

This salsa, submitted by Anne Crow, is a favorite of everyone who craves Tex-Mex food.

EL GRANDE SALSA

Makes 4 cups

2 [10–ounce] cans tomatoes and green chilies
4 torrida peppers
2 ripe tomatoes, peeled and chopped
4 green onions, chopped
1 teaspoon dried cilantro
Dash cumin
Dash oregano
Dash salt
Dash cracked pepper
Dash hot sauce
1 1/2 tablespoons vegetable oil
1 1/2 tablespoons red wine vinegar

- Put ingredients in a blender or food processor; pulse briefly to keep salsa chunky.
- Stores in refrigerator for up to 3 days.

Serve with Mexican food or corn chips

❧ PICANTE OLÉ

Makes 3 cups

1 [8–ounce] package cream cheese, softened
2 tablespoons dried onion soup mix
1 cup picante sauce, medium to hot

- Mix cream cheese and soup mix together in medium bowl, stirring until they are well blended.
- Stir in picante sauce.
- Serve with corn chips.

Freezes well

❧ TSATZIKI

(Greek Cucumber and Yogurt Dip)
Makes 2 1/2 cups

1 cup small-curd cottage cheese
1 medium cucumber, peeled, seeded, and chopped
4 green onions, chopped
2 to 4 cloves of garlic, finely chopped or pressed
1 cup plain yogurt
Salt to taste

- Purée cottage cheese, cucumber, onions, and garlic in a blender or food processor.
- Combine with yogurt.
- Add salt to taste.
- Store covered in refrigerator for 2 to 3 days.

Serve with toasted cut up pita bread, bagel chips, or raw vegetables. May also be used as topping for baked potatoes or as salad dressing.

27

❧ SHERRIED MUSHROOMS

Serves 4 as an appetizer

1/4 cup butter or margarine
1 pound small, whole fresh mushrooms
1/4 teaspoon paprika
1/4 teaspoon black pepper
1 teaspoon seasoned salt
2 tablespoons dry sherry
2 tablespoons chopped parsley
2 tablespoons chopped fresh herbs
2 tablespoons fresh grated Parmesan cheese

Conventional cooking:
• Heat butter in a skillet over medium heat for about 10 minutes.
• Add mushrooms, dry ingredients, and sherry. Sauté for about 10 minutes.
• Drain mushrooms and place on a platter or in individual ramekins.
• Sprinkle liberally with chopped parsley and other chopped fresh herbs, and grated Parmesan cheese.

To Grill:
• Place mushrooms in the center of a 24–inch square of heavy aluminum foil.
• Sprinkle with dry ingredients, and dot with butter. Add sherry.
• Loosely fold the foil into a package, folding ends over twice to seal foil securely.
• Put foil package seam side down at edge of grill, six inches above coals. Grill for 10 minutes; turn and grill an additional 10 minutes.
• Serve mushrooms in the foil; sprinkle liberally with chopped parsley and other chopped fresh herbs, and grated Parmesan cheese.

Also good as a side dish for beef.

❧ STUFFED MUSHROOMS

Makes 30 to 40 pieces; serves 12

30 to 40 mushrooms, washed and dried
10 slices bacon, cooked and crumbled
3/4 cup mayonnaise
1 small onion, chopped
1 1/2 cups [6 ounces] grated sharp Cheddar cheese
Dash seasoned salt

- Remove stems from mushrooms. Chop stems.
- Mix mayonnaise, bacon, onion, salt, and chopped mushroom stems together.
- Stuff mixture into mushroom caps.
- Top with grated cheese.
- Arrange mushrooms in a 9 x 13–inch baking dish and bake at 350° for 30minutes.

❧ TOMATOES STUFFED WITH FETA CHEESE

Serves 12 to 14

1 pint cherry tomatoes
1/2 cup olive oil
3 tablespoons white wine
1 teaspoon salt
1/2 teaspoon pepper
1 clove garlic, finely minced
4 ounces feta cheese
Fresh basil leaves

- Clean and core cherry tomatoes, making a depression 1/3 deep into each tomato.
- Mix olive oil, vinegar, salt, pepper, garlic, and basil to make a dressing.
- Pour dressing over tomatoes, tossing to coat well.
- Marinate tomatoes in refrigerator for several hours.
- Arrange tomatoes on a platter.
- Place about 1/2 teaspoon of feta cheese into depression in top of each tomato and place in a fresh basil leaf on top of cheese. (You can skewer leaf and cheese to tomatoes with toothpicks for easier handling, if you wish.)

29

Cosmo's Pizza was Birmingham's first gourmet pizza restaurant. Located in historic Five Points South, it offers a wide variety of dishes from contemporary Italian cuisine and traditional-style pizza to pizza of the 90s made with whole-wheat crust, sun-dried tomatoes, and goat cheese. A consistently popular restaurant, Cosmo's has given us their recipe for a unique and versatile roasted yellow pepper sauce you are sure to enjoy.

ROASTED YELLOW PEPPER SAUCE

Makes 2 cups

5 yellow peppers
2 teaspoons minced garlic
1 heaping tablespoon pine nuts
1/2 cup extra virgin olive oil
1/2 cup grated Parmesan cheese

- Roast and peel peppers.
- Blend peppers, garlic, and pine nuts in a food processor.
- Add oil in a slow, steady stream until it is completely incorporated into sauce. Fold in 1/2 cup grated Parmesan cheese.

Serve with warm pita, as a sauce on pizza, or over pasta.

VEGETABLE SANDWICHES

Makes 3 1/2 cups; enough for several dozen small sandwiches

1 envelope unflavored gelatin
1/4 cup water
1 cup diced celery
1/2 cup diced onion
3 small carrots, diced
1 green pepper, diced
1 teaspoon salt
Dash pepper
1 1/2 cups mayonnaise

- Soak gelatin in 1/4 cup water and dissolve over hot water.
- Mix remaining ingredients together and add to gelatin.
- Store mixture in refrigerator.
- When ready to use, make finger sandwiches by trimming crust from slice of bread. Cut each slice into three equal pieces. Repeat procedure until you have enough pieces for desired number of sandwiches.
- Spread approximately 1 tablespoon of mixture between two pieces of bread.
- Sandwiches can be made several hours ahead and stored in an air-tight container in the refrigerator.

Any unused sandwich mixture can be kept for days in the refrigerator.

GARDEN MEDLEY APPETIZER

Makes about 35 squares

2 packages [8 ounces] refrigerated crescent rolls
1 [8–ounce] package cream cheese, softened
2/3 cup mayonnaise
1 to 2 tablespoons minced onions
1 teaspoon dill weed
3 cups assorted raw vegetables, chopped and tossed (broccoli, green and red
   sweet pepper, green and black olives, tomatoes, celery, onion, etc.)

- Unroll crescent rolls, but do not separate them.
- Lay flat, covering the bottom of a 10 x 14–inch jelly roll pan; press edges
  together to seal seams.
- Bake according to package directions.
- Cool.
- Mix cream cheese, mayonnaise, and dill weed together. Spread mixture over
  baked crescents.
- Layer vegetables evenly on top.
- Cover and chill.
- Cut into 2–inch squares and serve.

Betty Kao is well known in Birmingham's culinary circles. The first to open a Chinese restaurant in the city, she has also taught cooking and done catering, and is presently sous chef at Vincent's Market. They have provided her most tantalizing Vegetable Sushi, easy to prepare and a delicious change from the ordinary.

 **VEGETABLE SUSHI**

Serves 12 to 16

4 1/2 cups short-grain rice
5 cups water
1/2 cup rice wine vinegar
2 tablespoons sugar
1 teaspoon salt
1 medium zucchini
1 medium carrot
2 stalks celery
1 bunch green onions
4 to 5 sheets seaweed
2 tablespoons washabi (Japanese horseradish)

Dipping sauce
2 tablespoons soy sauce
1 tablespoon rice wine
1/2 tablespoon sugar
1 teaspoon tapioca starch
1 teaspoon seasame oil

- Rinse the rice about 3 to 4 times until water is clear; add 5 cups water, then bring to a boil. Cover pot, reduce heat to low, and simmer 15 to 20 minutes.
- After rice is done, mix with rice wine vinegar, sugar, and salt. Stir well and set aside.
- Cut vegetables into thin strips.
- Place a seaweed on a bamboo mat. Spread 1/2 cup of rice over the seaweed to within about 2 inches of the edges.
- Smear 1/2 tablespoon washabi over the rice. Arrange vegetable strips along the center of the rice. Lift up the mat gently to roll the layers into a long, tight cylinder; the vegetables will form the center, surrounded by the rice, and wrapped in the seaweed.
- When all the sushi has been made, gently slice across it to form sections about 1–inch wide.

Serve with dipping sauce.

32

Josef Sudek (Czech, 1896–1976), *Glass and Lemon*, c. 1947, printed in 1950. Bromoil pigment print, 9 1/4 x 6 5/8 inches. Museum purchase with funds from The Photography Guild.

Josef Sudek, almost unknown in the West prior to the fall of the Iron Curtain, is now gaining recognition with the recent opening up of Eastern Europe. His photography is becoming well known thanks to numerous publications concerning his work and a series of major retrospectives in 1977–78 and 1982.

Best known for poetic single-tone landscapes and interior shots, he has also produced a number of exquisite still life images such as this one in the museum's permanent collection. Sudek's photographs are infused with moody, soft overtones and frequently involve the effects of combining light and water in the shots. In *Glass and Lemon*, we see the distortion of the shapes through the glass and water, a subtle reminder of how our own perception of reality is often distorted.

∾ CHEDDAR CHEESE OLIVE BALLS

Makes 48 balls

48 pitted ripe or stuffed green olives, or martini onions
1 cup all-purpose flour
1 teaspoon paprika
1/2 teaspoon salt
2 cups [8 ounces] grated Cheddar cheese
6 tablespoons butter or margarine, softened

- Drain and dry the olives or onions.
- Mix remaining ingredients together and knead mixture until it is the consistency of pie dough.
- Taking one teaspoonful of the mixture at a time, form dough into balls. Make a thumbprint in the center of each ball, and wrap dough around each olive or onion, covering completely.
- Place balls on a cookie sheet and freeze them. When frozen, place in a freezer container and return to freezer until ready to bake.
- To cook, place frozen balls on a cookie sheet and bake at 400° for 10 to 13 minutes.

Good make-ahead dish

CHEESE BITES

Makes 40 to 45 pieces

1 loaf unsliced French or sourdough bread (about 1 1/2 pounds)
1 [3–ounce] package cream cheese
1 cup [4 ounces] grated sharp Cheddar cheese
1/2 cup butter or margarine
2 egg whites

- Remove crust from bread and cut into 1–inch cubes using an electric knife.
- Melt cheese and butter in a double boiler until mixture is the consistency of rarebit, stirring often. Remove from heat.
- Beat egg whites in a food processor. Remove the stopper from the feeder tube of the processor. With processor running, carefully pour melted cheese mixture down the tube into the stiff egg whites until mixture is well blended.
- Using two fondue forks, dip bread cubes, one at a time, in the cheese mixture. Let excess cheese drip from each cube, then dry on a wax paper-lined cookie sheet. To speed drying, place cubes in freezer for 1/2 hour.
- When cubes are thoroughly dry, trim excess "drippings" from cubes, and store them in plastic bags in freezer until needed.
- Place frozen cubes on lightly-greased baking sheets, defrost for 1/2 hour, and bake at 450° for 5 to 10 minutes, until lightly browned.
- Serve hot.

Good make-ahead dish

 **COFFEE PUNCH**

Serves 25

1 gallon strong coffee (11 tablespoons for 30–cup percolator)
Pinch of salt
1/2 teaspoon cinnamon
1 cup sugar
1/2 cup chocolate syrup
1/2 gallon vanilla or coffee ice cream

- Make the coffee in a 30–cup percolator (or make enough strong coffee to equal 1 gallon). Cool and place in a 5–quart container.
- Add the salt, cinnamon, sugar, and chocolate syrup; mix well. Cover and refrigerate.
- To serve, place the ice cream in a punch bowl and pour the coffee mixture over it. The ice cream may be used in scoops or blocks.

FANTASIA PUNCH

Makes 3 quarts

1 [6–ounce] can frozen orange juice
1 [6–ounce] can frozen lemonade
1 [6–ounce] can frozen limeade
1 [46–ounce] can pink grapefruit juice
1 [46–ounce] can pineapple juice
1 quart bottle of light rum

- Mix all ingredients in a covered container. Place in freezer.
- Stir mixture well after 24 hours, and return it to freezer until it becomes a thick slush.
- Place in a punch bowl over ice and serve.

SOUPS

(Page 37) Tureen with Stand, Niderviller (France) ca. 1754–70. Tin-glazed earthenware (faience) with colored enamel decoration. The tureen and lid: 9 3/4 x 14 5/8 x 8 9/16 inches; the stand: 1 3/8 x 21 1/2 x 14 3/16 inches. Eugenia Woodward Hitt Collection.

The animated sculptural shape of this tureen and stand exemplifies the imaginative tablewares produced at Niderviller in the 1750s. The tureen combines the rococo vocabulary of lively scrolls and shellwork with three-dimensional mushrooms, leeks, mollusks, and artichokes, modelled from life and painted in vibrant, naturalistic enamel colors. Niderviller employed the revolutionary new *petit feu* (low fired) technique for painted decoration. The lower kiln temperature required for *petit feu* decorations allowed for a wider, brighter color palette, apparent here in the greens, blues, purples, and *poupre de Cassius* (named for the Dutch chemist who discovered this pink-purple).

38

HOT SOUPS

CHILLED SOUPS

〜 MUSTARD SOUP

Serves 4 to 6

2 tablespoons butter
3 tablespoons prepared mustard (Dijon-style is excellent)
2 tablespoons flour
2 1/2 cups skimmed chicken stock, heated
1 1/4 cups light cream or half-and-half
1/2 teaspoon salt
Dash of white pepper
1/2 teaspoon onion juice
2 egg yolks
2 to 3 tablespoons heavy cream

- Melt the butter, stir in flour and blend smoothly.
- Add hot chicken stock and milk and whisk until smooth.
- Add salt, pepper, and onion juice.
- Simmer for 10 to 15 minutes; cool slightly.
- Combine egg yolks and cream and add to the soup, first adding a few spoonfuls of the warm broth to the egg mixture.
- Stir in the mustard and cook over low heat until heated through and thickened.

Can be served hot or chilled; if served hot, garnish with green peas; chilled, with a dab of whipped cream.

Dating from the time of Charles V of France, this unusual soup is a gourmet delight fit for a king. Made with one of Europe's favorite spices from before the middle ages right up to the present, the recipe was originally published in *Le Viandier*, which was compiled by Guillaume Tirel (Taillevent) about 1375 for the court of Charles V. After trying it, we found that the dish is timeless, as delicious now as it was in the fourteenth century. The recipe is from *The Delectable Past*.

The Back Alley Restaurant was among the first Birmingham restaurants to offer outdoor dining and has become a year-round favorite, not only for the pleasant ambiance, but also for their superb cuisine. They have one of the most extensive soup menus in town, offering a different choice every day. One of the all-time favorites is Artichoke-Oyster soup.

❧ ARTICHOKE-OYSTER SOUP

Serves 4 to 6

1/4 cup butter
1 clove garlic, pressed
1/4 cup finely chopped onions
1/4 cup finely chopped carrots
1 cup sliced mushrooms
1 [14–ounce] can artichoke hearts
1 [14 1/2–ounce] can chicken stock
1/2 cup dry white wine
1/2 teaspoon lemon pepper
Salt and pepper to taste
2 teaspoons Worcestershire sauce
Dash hot sauce
1/2 pound shucked fresh oysters
2 cups half-and-half
1 to 2 tablespoons all-purpose flour mixed with 3 to 4 tablespoons water, if necessary

- Melt butter in stock pot and sauté garlic, carrots, mushrooms, onions, and artichoke hearts for 3 to 5 minutes.
- Add chicken broth, wine, lemon pepper, salt, pepper, Worcestershire sauce, and hot sauce and cook until carrots are tender, about 20 to 30 minutes.
- Add oysters and heat until oysters are cooked and the edges begin to curl, about 5 minutes.
- Stir in half-and-half and heat through.
- If it is necessary to thicken soup, mix the flour and water to make a paste and whisk into the soup, stirring until thickened.

❧ LOW COUNTRY CAROLINA CHICKEN AND SHRIMP GUMBO

Serves 10 to 14

1/2 cup margarine
1 cup thinly sliced celery
1/2 cup chopped green pepper
1/2 cup chopped onion
1 cup canned tomatoes
1 cup whole kernel corn
1/2 cup finely chopped parsley
10 cups water
1/2 teaspoon garlic powder
1/2 teaspoon basil
1 tablespoon Kitchen Bouquet
3/4 teaspoon Old Bay seasoning
1/2 teaspoon seasoning salt
1/4 teaspoon white pepper
2 tablespoons Worcestershire sauce
3 tablespoons gumbo filé
1/2 box Knorr Swiss Clam Chowder base
2 [16–ounce] packages frozen okra
1 1/4 pounds 40/50 count shrimp
2 1/2 pounds chicken breasts, cut into 1– to 2–inch cubes
2 to 3 tablespoons vegetable oil for cooking chicken

• Sauté vegetables in margarine in a large cooking pot.
• Add water and slowly bring to a boil. Add chowder mix, spices, okra, shrimp, and all other ingredients except chicken.
• Sauté chicken in vegetable oil, then add to base.
• Turn down heat and simmer for 3 minutes. Remove from heat.

May be served over rice.
Recipe can be halved.

Cabana Café has moved its location several times over the last fifteen years, now residing in Wildwood Center, but the menu has remained consistently delicious. With a strong emphasis on seafood and contemporary Southern cooking, Cabana Café has remained one of Birmingham's most popular restaurants. Low Country Carolina Chicken and Shrimp Gumbo combines seafood and Southern cuisine in a dish everyone will love.

This recipe is for a tasty genuine Cajun gumbo for all those with a robust appetite. It was submitted by Thomas Kirkland who spends up to an hour slowly developing the roux.

42

❧ SHRIMP, CRAB, AND SAUSAGE GUMBO

Serves 8 to 12

1/2 cup cooking oil
1/2 cup all-purpose flour
1 large onion, chopped
2 to 3 cloves garlic, minced
1 1/2 green peppers, chopped
3 stalks celery, chopped
8 green onions, chopped
1 pound whole tomatoes, fresh or canned, undrained, coarsely chopped
1 1/2 pounds frozen okra
Oil for frying okra (2 to 3 tablespoons)
2 [10 3/4–ounce] cans chicken stock, plus three cans hot water
2 tablespoons salt
1/2 to 3/4 teaspoon red pepper
1 large bay leaf
1/4 teaspoon thyme
8 to 10 allspice berries
1 pound crab claw meat (crab claws peeled for appetizers)
2 pounds raw headless shrimp, peeled
1 pound smoked sausage
1 pound lump crab meat
1/2 cup chopped green onions
1/2 cup chopped parsley
Cooked rice, 1/2 cup per person

- Heat 1/2 cup cooking oil in a heavy 8–quart stock pot over medium heat. Slowly sprinkle flour into oil, stirring constantly with a wooden spoon to keep flour from sticking to bottom of pot. Continue to add flour and stir until it is a rich, dark caramel brown.
- Add onion, garlic, green pepper, celery, and green onions, and cook slowly until onions are transparent.
- Add tomatoes and cook on low heat, stirring frequently, until oil rises to top.
- In a separate skillet, fry okra in 2 to 3 tablespoons of oil over medium high heat, stirring constantly.
- Preheat oven to 400°. Cut sausage into small pieces and wrap them in aluminum foil. Bake 20 minutes.
- Add okra and sausage to the mixture; stir and simmer for about 10 minutes.

- Add chicken stock, water, salt, and pepper; simmer partially covered for 45 minutes.
- Add bay leaf, thyme, allspice berries, and crab claw meat, and simmer for 20 minutes.
- Add shrimp and crabmeat, and simmer 15 more minutes.
- Taste; correct seasonings if necessary.
- Remove from heat, and stir in 1/2 cup chopped green onions and parsley.
- Serve over rice.

A pint of oysters may also be used; add during last 5 minutes of cooking. Variations may be made by using different seafood, sausage, or poultry.

❧ FISH CHOWDER

Serves 6 to 8

1/2 cup butter or margarine
1/2 medium onion, sliced
2 cups fish stock or water
2 cups potatoes, peeled and diced
1 pound fish cut into small pieces
   (Fish choices: shrimp, clam, whitefish, etc.)
1 teaspoon each, salt and pepper
2 tablespoons butter or margarine
2 tablespoons all-purpose flour
1 teaspoon paprika
3 cups milk, scalded
Parsley for garnish

- Melt 1/2 cup butter in a 4–quart sauce pan.
- Sauté onions for 5 minutes until brown.
- Add stock or water, potatoes, fish, and salt and pepper.
- Cook until potatoes are soft.
- Melt two tablespoons of butter in a skillet or sauce pan. Add flour and paprika, and stir until smooth. Add milk and stir until sauce boils.
- Add sauce to soup stock, and bring to a boil. Correct seasonings if necessary.
- Serve hot with parsley garnish.

43

❧ PANTRY GUMBO

Serves 4

3 tablespoons butter
3/4 cup chopped celery
3/4 cup chopped green pepper
1/2 cup chopped green onion
1 tablespoon parsley
1 bay leaf
1 [10 1/2–ounce] can mushroom soup
1 [15 1/2–ounce] can okra
1 [16–ounce can] tomatoes, chopped
12 ounces fresh or frozen shrimp, peeled
1/2 cup water
1/2 teaspoon salt
Dash black pepper
Dash cayenne pepper
1 teaspoon filé powder
2 cups cooked rice

- Melt butter in a large pot.
- Sauté celery, green pepper, onion, parsley, and bay leaf until tender.
- Blend remaining ingredients, except filé powder and rice, and add to vegetable mixture.
- Heat to boiling, remove from heat, and stir in filé powder just before serving.
- Add rice to the gumbo, or put 1/2 cup of rice into each soup bowl and top with gumbo.

◡ PESTO TORTELLINI SOUP

Serves 4 to 6

6 ounces spinach tortellini, stuffed with cheese
4 cups chicken broth
2 cups heavy cream
1 cup pesto sauce (recipe follows)
Fresh basil leaves for garnish

- Cook tortellini according to package directions; drain.
- Place broth, cream, and pesto sauce in a large sauce pan, stir, and simmer for 5 minutes.
- Add tortellini and continue simmering until just bubbly; do not boil or overcook pasta.
- Serve with basil leaf garnish.

Keeps several days in refrigerator.

Pesto Sauce

Makes 1 cup

1 cup fresh basil leaves, firmly packed (or use 1/4 cup dried basil plus 1/4 cup fresh chopped parsley. Use less garlic and add up to 2 additional tablespoons of lemon juice)
3 to 6 cloves garlic
1 cup freshly grated Parmesan cheese
1/4 cup pine nuts
1 tablespoon lemon juice
1/2 cup extra virgin olive oil
Salt and pepper to taste

- Put the basil, garlic, cheese, pine nuts, and lemon juice in a food processor or blender. Add olive oil drop by drop until the sauce is the consistency of mayonnaise.

45

 **PASTA MEATBALL SOUP**

Serves 4 to 6

1 pound ground chuck
6 tablespoons dry bread crumbs
Salt and pepper to taste
2 tablespoons butter or margarine
1/2 to 1 cup sliced green onions
1 1/2 teaspoons parsley flakes
6 cups water
6 beef bouillon cubes
1 [5–ounce] package fine egg noodles
Fresh chopped parsley to taste
Grated Parmesan cheese

- Mix meat, bread crumbs, salt, and pepper, and shape into balls.
- Brown meatballs in butter in a large pot.
- Remove meatballs and set them aside.
- Brown onions in same pot.
- Add water and bouillon cubes, and bring to a boil to dissolve cubes.
- Add noodles to boiling broth and cook, stirring, for 5 minutes.
- Add meatballs and cook for about 8 minutes, stirring occasionally.
- Sprinkle with chopped parsley and Parmesan cheese and serve.

Good with tossed salad and bread.

46

Mrs. Percy Brower submitted this recipe which she likes because it is thickened with cabbage rather than the higher calorie, starchy potato. It is a favorite of her children who love to take home the leftovers to serve over pasta.

HEARTY ITALIAN SOUP

Serves 10

2 pounds Italian sausage
2 tablespoons olive oil
2 cups chopped onion
4 cloves garlic, minced
1 1/2 cups sliced carrots
2 teaspoons dried basil, crumbled
1 [28–ounce] can crushed tomatoes
3 cups beef broth
2 1/2 cups grated cabbage
Pepper to taste
4 small zucchini, peeled and sliced
1 [16–ounce] can Great Northern beans

- Place the sausage in a large ovenproof pot, cover with water, and boil for 10 minutes. Place in the oven and bake at 350° for 30 minutes, until most of fat cooks out. Remove the sausage and discard the liquid. Slice sausage into thin slices, place them on a broiler pan, and broil until lightly browned on both sides. Set aside.
- Sauté onions and garlic in olive oil.
- Place onions, garlic, carrots, basil, tomatoes, broth, cabbage, and pepper in a soup pot. Cook for 1 hour.
- Brush the zucchini with olive oil and brown lightly in the oven broiler. Add zucchini, beans, and sausage to soup pot and simmer for 20 minutes more.

May be frozen.

ONIONS MONAGASQUE

Serves 4 to 6

1 [6–ounce] can tomato paste
1/4 cup canola oil
2 pounds Vidalia onions, chopped or sliced
2 3/4 cups water
1/2 cup red wine vinegar
3/4 cup golden raisins
1/4 cup brown sugar
2 bay leaves
1 teaspoon dried thyme
1/2 cup chopped fresh parsley
Salt and pepper to taste

- Place all ingredients, except onions, in a large sauce pan and bring to a boil.
- Reduce heat; add onions and simmer for 30 minutes.
- Remove bay leaves and serve.

47

This recipe comes from the museum's assisstant curator of Traditional Arts, Mary Villadsen. Mary loves natural foods and is an excellent cook. One day she was looking for a good soup recipe with natural ingredients and was having no luck finding one. She solved the problem by coming up with her own recipe. We are now happy to pass this tantalizing and delicious soup recipe on to you.

∾ POTATO CHEESE SOUP

Serves 8 to 10

3 to 4 tablespoons unsalted butter (may use half olive oil)
3 to 4 cups chopped white onions
2 cloves garlic, minced or pressed
6 to 8 medium red potatoes, scrubbed, unpeeled,
    and chopped into small cubes
2 to 3 carrots, scrubbed, unpeeled, and chopped
3 to 4 cups vegetable stock or water
6 to 8 ounces cream cheese
2 cups milk
2 cups grated yellow cheese (sharp Cheddar, colby, etc.)
2 tablespoons fresh dill or 1 teaspoon dried dill
Salt and freshly ground pepper to taste
Chopped fresh parsley for garnish

- In a large pot, sauté onions and garlic in melted butter (or oil) until they are translucent.
- Add potatoes and carrots and sauté 10 to15 minutes longer.
- Cover with stock or water and simmer until potatoes are tender.
- In a blender or food processor, purée potato mixture with cream cheese and milk. (If planning to freeze, stop at this step.)
- Return puréed mixture to pot, and stir in yellow cheese and dill.
- Reheat gently. Do not boil or cheese may curdle and lump.
- Serve with fresh parsley garnish.

For spicier soup, use hot pepper flakes instead of dill. Can be frozen.

∾ VEGETABLE AND CHEESE BISQUE

Serves 4 to 5

1 cup thinly sliced leeks
1 cup thinly sliced fresh mushrooms
3 tablespoons butter
3 tablespoons flour
3 cups chicken stock
2 cups small broccoli florets
1 cup half-and-half
1 1/2 cups shredded Jarlsburg cheese

- Sauté leeks and mushrooms in buter until tender.
- Add flour and cook for 1 minute, stirring constantly.
- Add chicken stock, stirring until thick and smooth.
- Add broccoli, reduce heat and simmer for 20 minutes.
- Stir in half-and-half.
- Add cheese and blend. Continue simmering, stirring occassionally, until cheese is melted, being careful not to boil.
- Serve immediately.

❧ CREAM CHEESE AND OLIVE SOUP

Makes 6 to 8 servings (8 cups)

3 slices bacon
2 tablespoons butter
1/2 cup finely chopped onion
1/2 cup finely chopped celery hearts
1/2 cup finely chopped red bell pepper
1/4 cup flour
3 cups chicken stock or broth
2 cups half-and-half
1 [8–ounce] package cream cheese, cut into 1/2–inch pieces
1/2 cup minced green olives

- In a heavy 3–quart stock pot, fry bacon over meduim heat till crisp. Remove from pot and set aside to cool.
- Add butter to bacon fat in pot, then add the chopped vegetables. Cook, stirring, for 3 minutes.
- Add the flour and cook, stirring, 3 minutes more.
- Slowly add the chicken broth, stirring with a whisk so that no lumps remain.
- Stir in the half-and-half, increase heat to medium, and continue to cook, stirring, until it comes to a gentle boil.
- Add cream cheese pieces and stir with a whisk until the cream cheese is completely melted.
- Stir in olives.
- Ladle into bowls, garnish with crumbled bacon, and serve.

Fox Valley is a relative newcomer to the Birmingham restaurant scene, but it has quickly gained a reputation as one of the area's finest restaurants. Located south of the city in Maylene, Fox Valley's menu runs from the traditional hamburger to roast duck, with the quality of the food making it well worth the drive. Their contribution to this cookbook offers a new twist on a favorite Southern luncheon item, the cream cheese and olive sandwich. The combination of these ingredients, along with several others, forms a cleverly unique and absolutely delicious Cream Cheese and Olive Soup.

49

❧ FROSTY CUCUMBER SOUP

Serves 4

1 [10 3/4–ounce] can condensed cream of asparagus soup
1/2 cup sour cream
1/2 cup small curd cottage cheese
1 medium cucumber, peeled, seeded, and chopped
1 teaspoon minced onion
1/4 teaspoon dried dill
Salt and pepper to taste
1/2 cucumber, seeded and chopped
1/4 cup chopped celery
Dill or parsley sprigs

- Place first 6 ingredients in a blender container; cover and process at medium speed until mixture is puréed.
- Pour into a 1–quart covered container.
- Add salt and pepper.
- Add 1/2 cup chopped cucumber and 1/4 cup chopped celery to container.
- Chill until very cold.
- Serve garnished with parsley sprig.

50

∿ VICHYSSOISE

Serves 12

1/4 cup butter or margarine
3 or 4 leeks, cleaned, halved, and thinly sliced
1 or 2 small onions, finely chopped
2 or 3 medium baking potatoes, peeled and sliced (Let the slices set in cold
   water until ready to use to prevent discoloring.)
2 [14 1/2–ounce] cans chicken broth
1 teaspoon salt
2 to 3 dashes white pepper
2 cups half-and-half
1 cup milk
Fresh chopped chives for garnish

- Melt butter in a large soup pot. Sauté leeks and onions until they are soft, being careful not to burn. Add potatoes, broth, salt, and pepper. Bring to a boil.
- Reduce heat to low and cook, covered, for 45 minutes or until potatoes are soft. Cool.
- Break potatoes with a fork.
- Blend mixture in a food processor, about 2 cups at a time, until it is smooth. Put through strainer, if necessary. Chill.
- When ready to serve, slowly add the half-and-half, stirring with a wire whisk. Add milk until soup reaches desired consistency.
- Serve cold in chilled bowls, garnished with chives.

Variation: Add 4 medium cucumbers, peeled, seeded, and chopped.

51

SUNSHINE SQUASH SOUP

Serves 4

1 pound yellow squash, thinly sliced
2/3 cup chopped onion
2 cups chicken broth
1/4 cup sour cream
3 drops hot sauce
Salt and white pepper to taste

- In a 1 1/2–quart sauce pan, combine squash, onion, and 1 cup of broth. Bring to a boil.
- Cover and simmer for 30 minutes.
- Cool, then purée mixture in a blender.
- Transfer to a bowl.
- Add remaining broth, sour cream, and seasonings.
- Refrigerate at least 4 hours before serving.

SUMMER TOMATO SOUP

Serves 6

4 cups canned condensed tomato soup
1 cup light cream or skim milk
1 tablespoon grated onion
1/4 teaspoon hot sauce
1 pinch of lemon dill or dill
Salt and pepper to taste
1/2 cup sour cream or plain yogurt
1 tablespoon chopped parsley

- Mix soup, light cream, onion, hot sauce, lemon dill, salt, and pepper.
- Chill overnight in refrigerator.
- When ready to serve, stir in the sour cream.
- Serve cold in chilled bowls, garnished with parsley.

52

❧ CHILLED ZUCCHINI SOUP

Serves 6 to 8

5 medium zucchini, thinly sliced
1 large onion, thinly sliced
1 1/2 teaspoons curry powder
3 cups canned chicken broth
1 1/2 cups half-and-half or milk
Salt to taste
Pepper to taste
Fresh chopped chives for garnish

- Place zucchini, onion, and curry powder in a 4–quart sauce pan.
- Add chicken broth and stir well.
- Bring to a boil. Reduce heat, cover, and simmer about 45 minutes. Cool.
- Purée cooled mixture in a blender.
- Stir in half-and-half, salt, and pepper.
- Chill and serve with chopped chives for garnish.

❧ GASPACHO

Serves 6

3 fresh tomatoes, peeled, seeded, and chopped
1 large cucumber, peeled, seeded, and chopped
1 1/2 green peppers, sliced
1 small onion, diced
1 slice white bread
1/2 teaspoon minced garlic
3 cups tomato juice
2 tablespoons red wine vinegar
1 tablespoon olive oil

- Combine tomatoes, cucumber, bell pepper, and onion, reserving 6 tablespoons of the mixture for garnish.
- Put chopped vegetables, bread, and remaining ingredients into a food processor or blender and process until they are smooth.
- Chill. (After a day in the refrigerator, the soup gets very thick.)
- Garnish each serving with 1 tablespoon of the reserved vegetable mixture.

Mrs. Bernard Steiner, who submitted this recipe for Chilled Zucchini Soup, says it is an elegant and delicious soup for company. She recommends using half-and-half, and adds that the recipe is easy or she couldn't make it.

53

This authentic Swedish dish was submitted by Mrs. Eivor H. Callahan. She relates that dried fruit was often used in Swedish cooking because fresh fruit was not readily available throughout much of the year in her home country.

 **SWEDISH FRUIT SOUP**

Serves 6 to 8

1 [6–ounce] package dried apricots
1 [6–ounce] package dried prunes
1 tablespoon dried currants
2 tablespoons raisins
6 cups cold water
1 stick cinnamon
2 lemon slices, 1/4 inch thick
3 tablespoons quick tapioca or cornstarch
1 cup sugar
1 tart apple, peeled, cored, and cut in 1/2–inch slices

• Soak dried fruits in cold water for 30 minutes.
• Mix all ingredients together, including water used to soak fruits.
• Cook over medium heat for 30 minutes.
• Serve hot or cold, as a soup or dessert course.

Good when topped with sour cream or yogurt

EGGS, CHEESE &BRUNCH

(Page 55) Claude Monet, (French, 1840–1926), *Le Matin, Temps Brumeux, Pourville,* 1882. Oil on canvas, 24 x 29 1/8 inches. Museum purchase with funds provided by the 1978 and 1980–83 Beaux Arts Committees.

Like many impressionist works, this scene was most likely quickly painted outdoors in one session, rather than in the artist's studio from studies done outdoors. The aim of the impressionists was to capture the transitory effects of light in their canvases. In this painting of the cliffs at Pourville, Monet was interested in transcription rather than interpretation, seeing himself as an objective recorder of the scene before him. He avoided the suggestion of human presence in his later works, stressing, rather, nature and the elements. Like many of the impressionists, he used easily discernible brushstrokes in vibrant colors, juxtaposed so that at a distance they would blend together to replicate the shimmering effect of natural light. Monet was best known for his landscapes and floral paintings, frequently doing serial paintings of the same scene or setting at different times of the day or year to record the effects of the changing light.

56

EGGS, CHEESE, AND BRUNCH

❧ SPINACH PECAN QUICHE

Serves 8

1 10–inch unbaked pastry shell
6 eggs
2 cups heavy cream
1 1/2 cups grated Swiss cheese
1 cup ricotta cheese
1/4 cup grated Parmesan cheese
1 1/2 cups chopped, cooked spinach, well drained
1/2 cup chopped pecans
1 to 2 teaspoons salt
1/2 teaspoon pepper (preferably white)
1/2 teaspoon sugar
2 teaspoons dried dill weed
1/2 teaspoon dry mustard
1/2 teaspoon powdered ginger

• Preheat oven to 400°. To prevent shrinking, prick the bottom and sides of pastry shell with fork. Bake shell until lightly browned, 5 to 8 minutes.
• Remove shell from oven and reduce temperature to 350°.
• In a large mixing bowl, combine ingredients in order given, mixing well after each addition.
• Pour into partially baked pasty shell and bake until firm, about 45 to 55 minutes.

Our first recipe for this section comes from Meadowlark Farm restaurant in Alabaster. A pleasant drive south of town, this restaurant has gained the reputation for being one of the finest and most romantic in the area. Located in a pastoral setting in a converted farmhouse, Meadowlark Farm's greastest asset is the food. The menu varies according to season, and relies on the best ingredients available. These are prepared in the finest European tradition by chefs Nick Cairns and Karen York. They have shared with us a delicious Spinach and Pecan Quiche.

MAGIC CITY QUICHE

Serves 6

2 cups [8 ounces] shredded natural Swiss cheese
2 tablespoons all-purpose flour
1 1/2 cups half-and-half
4 eggs, lightly beaten
3/4 cup chopped, cooked shrimp or ham
1/2 teaspoon salt
Pepper to taste
1 9–inch unbaked pastry shell

• Toss cheese with the flour.
• Add half-and-half, eggs, shrimp or ham, and seasonings. Mix well.
• Pour into a pastry shell.
• Bake at 350° for 55 to 60 mintues, or until set.

Freezes well.

This recipe, from *The Delectable Past,* is from *L'Escole Parfaite des Officiers de Bouche,* which was published in France in 1662 as a guide for the households of French nobility. It gave information on foods and how to serve them to royalty, a result of Louis XIV's emphasis on fine cuisine and protocol. Oeufs à l'Intrigue is an interesting variation on our present-day Quiche Lorraine.

OEUFS À L'INTRIGUE

Serves 6

1 9–inch pastry, baked at 400° for 5 minutes
4 large eggs
3/4 cup cream
1/2 cup flaked crab meat or 1 [2–ounce] can anchovy fillets
1/4 cup grated Parmesan cheese
1/2 cup grated Swiss cheese
1 tablespoon grated onion
Salt and pepper to taste

• Beat the eggs with the cream until well blended, then add the grated onion.
• Pour 1/3 of the mixture into the baked pastry shell and bake at 400° for 5 minutes to allow the egg mixture to partially set.
• Remove from oven. Arrange crabmeat or anchovies on top of egg mixture and carefully spoon on another third of the eggs.
• Return to oven for 5 minutes, or until second layer begins to set.
• Remove from oven, sprinkle cheeses over top and spoon on last third of eggs.
• Return to oven and bake 20 minutes, or until nicely buffed and browned on top.

A delicious lunch entrée or first course.

58

(Left, on table) Vase, Germany, c. 1728–30, Porcelain, Meissen ware, 10 x 6 inches. Gift of the Estate of Francis Oliver.

(Left, on floor) Ogata Kenzan (1663–1743), Dish, Japan, Edo period (1615–1868). Glazed stoneware, 6 1/2 x 6 5/8 inches. Gift of Mr. and Mrs. Elton B. Stephens.

(Second from left, on floor) Dish, Japan, Edo period (1615–1868). Porcelain, Nabeshima ware, 7/8 x 4 11/16 inches. Gift of Mr. and Mrs. Albert L. Fairley, Jr.

(Second from right, on floor) Teapot, Japan, Edo period (1615–1868). Porcelain and gilt bronze, Kakiemon ware, 4 x 6 inches. Gift of Dr. and Mrs. Thomas Allen.

(Right, on floor) Jar, Japan, Edo period (1615–1868). Porcelain, Kakiemon ware, 11 1/2 x 9 1/8 inches. Gift of Mr. and Mrs. Harris Saunders.

Table, China, Qing dynasty (1644–1912). Wood, fabric, and lacquer. Gift of Dr. and Mrs. Norton T. Montague, Dr. and Mrs. Alvaro Ronderos, Mr. and Mrs. Doug Wiley, and Dr. and Mrs. Thomas Wilson.

Japanese ceramics had a profound influence on European wares when they began to be imported in large numbers during the seventeenth century. The delightful palette and decorations of Kakiemon porcelains were particularly popular, and were widely copied by Meissen and many other porcelain factories that began production in Europe at this time. Nabeshima ware and the work of such artists as Ogata Kenzan were originally not exported and came to be appreciated by Western connoisseurs only later.

◖ BREAKFAST SOUFFLÉ

Serves 8 to 10

1 1/2 pounds bulk sausage
9 eggs, well beaten
3 cups milk
1 1/2 teaspoons dry mustard
1 teaspoon salt
3 slices white bread, cut in 1/2-inch cubes
1 1/2 cups [6 ounces] shredded Cheddar cheese

- Cook sausage over medium heat until done; crumble into small pieces.
- Drain well on paper towels and set aside.
- Combine remaining ingredients and add sausage.
- Pour mixture into a well-greased 13 x 9 x 2-inch baking dish or a large soufflé dish. Cover and refrigerate overnight.
- Bake at 350° for 1 hour.

It is recommended that hot sausage and sharp cheese be used for maximum taste!
This is a wonderfully easy breakfast for overnight guests, as it can be prepared the day before. Serve with blueberry muffins, orange juice, and coffee for a superb breakfast.
Leftovers can be reheated in the microwave. Makes a nice lunch with a green salad and rolls.

This recipe is said to be the traditional brunch dish served at the Kentucky governor's mansion on Derby Day. We found the use of hard-boiled eggs in this casserole an unusual change from most breakfast or brunch dishes. For those who are worried about too much fat, we found it to be equally delicious without the crushed chips, and so mark them optional.

◖ DERBY DAY CASSEROLE

Serves 8 to 10

1/2 cup chopped onion
2 tablespoons butter
1 cup shredded sharp Cheddar cheese
2 tablespoons flour
6 hard-boiled eggs
1 1/4 cup milk
1 1/2 cup crushed potato chips (optional)
8 to 10 slices cooked bacon, crumbled

- Sauté onions in butter until they are translucent, but not brown.
- Add flour and stir until well blended; add milk and cook, stirring constantly, until mixture is thick.
- Add cheese and stir until melted.
- Place a layer of egg slices in the bottom of a 6 x 10–inch glass baking dish; cover with half the cheese sauce and half the crushed chips and crumbled bacon. Repeat layering.
- Bake at 350° for about 30 minutes until top is golden and casserole is bubbly.

Crushed chips may be omitted, or you may substitute the top layer with 1/4 cup dry bread crumbs mixed with 1 tablespoon melted butter.

❧ BEAUVILLIERS' CHEESE SOUFFLÉ

Serves 4 to 6

4 tablespoons butter
1/4 cup flour
1/8 teaspoon salt
1 1/2 cups scalded milk
1 cup grated Swiss cheese
1 cup grated Parmesan cheese
1/8 tablespoon grated nutmeg
4 eggs, separated

- Melt the butter in a saucepan, blend in the flour and salt, then add hot milk. Stir quickly with the wire whisk until thoroughly blended.
- Cool for a few minutes, then add the cheese, stirring to melt.
- Beat in the egg yolks, one at a time.
- Beat the egg whites until stiff, but not dry.
- Turn the egg whites into the cheese mixture; cut and fold lightly, only enough to blend.
- Turn into a 2–quart ungreased soufflé dish and bake at 375° for 35 minutes.
- Serve immediately.

Antoine Beauvilliers, one of the best known names in the history of French cuisine, resided in England during the French Revolution. Upon his return to Paris, he published *L'Art du Cuisinier* (1814), a two-volume guide to the best of English cooking. It includes one of the first recipes for cheese soufflé, so delicious that it has changed little in the intervening 180 years. This recipe is from *The Delectable Past*.

61

Dexter's on Hollywood is synonymous with fine dining in the Birmingham area. The mention of Dexter's also brings to mind their popular Saturday brunches, and this recipe is an excellent example of why. A New Orleans classic, Eggs Sardou at Dexter's Saturday brunch conjures up relaxing thoughts of the Big Easy and its unsurpassed cuisine. We offer you the next best thing to being served this delicious dish at Dexter's on a sunny, lazy Saturday morning: the recipe.

62

❧ EGGS SARDOU
Serves 4

1 1/4 pounds fresh spinach
1 1/2 cups whipping cream
1/4 teaspoon garlic
1/4 teaspoon white pepper
1/4 teaspoon salt
1 1/2 teaspoons Ouzo
2 English muffins, halved
4 poached eggs
4 artichoke bottoms
Hollandaise Sauce (recipe follows)

- Combine spinach, cream, garlic, white pepper, and salt in a large sauce pan.
- Reduce by 1/3, add Ouzo and stir.
- Toast English muffin halves and place on platter.
- Grill artichoke bottoms.
- Spoon about 2 tablespoons spinach mixture onto each muffin half and place artichoke bottom on top.
- Add poached egg and top with hollandaise.
- Serve with cheese grits and a fruit cup.

Hollandaise Sauce
Makes 3/4 cup

4 egg yolks
3 tablespoons hot water
2 tablespoons lemon juice
Salt and freshly ground pepper to taste
1/2 cup butter

- In the top of a double boiler or in a pan over simmering (not boiling) water, beat the egg yolks with a wire whisk until they are thick and pale in color.
- Add the hot water, lemon juice, and salt and pepper, and beat vigorously.
- Divide the butter into thirds, and add first portion to pan. Continue to whisk until butter is melted and mixture begins to thicken. Add second portion, then third, beating constantly. Stir and cook until thickened, being careful not to overcook or mixture will curdle.
- If mixture begins to curdle, place pan over ice and stir vigorously; or remove from heat and add 2 tablespoons cold cream and beat quickly.

Recipe makes about 2 cups of spinach filling. Leftover filling can be refrigerated and used with fish, chicken, veal, or vegetables as a stuffing.

BAKED TOMATO AND POTATO OMLETTE

Serves 4

4 tablespoons butter
1 large onion, finely chopped
1 large baking potato
2 tablespoons lemon juice
2 large tomatoes, sliced
1/2 teaspoon salt
1/4 teaspoon pepper
4 eggs
1/4 teaspoon salt
1/4 teaspoon cinnamon

- Melt butter in a skillet and sauté onion until golden.
- With a slotted spoon, transfer onion to a bowl add lemon juice and let stand.
- Pare and slice potato in 1/4–inch thick slices; wash well in cold water.
- Dry slices and fry until golden in same skillet.
- Arrange tomatoes over potatoes and add onions.
- Season with 1/2 teaspoon salt and 1/4 teaspoon pepper.
- Cover and let simmer for 10 minutes over low heat.
- Beat eggs with salt and cinnamon.
- Pour over contents of skillet, cover, and let cook over low heat for another
  10 minutes.
- Serve immediately.

This dish does not freeze or work in the microwave.
When served with bread and salad, this dish makes a delicious brunch, lunch, or light supper.

63

TO MAKE A SHRIMP AUMLET

Shell as many shrimp as will fill a pint [*1 cup, about 1/2 pound*], and chop them a little; add a handful of parsly [*1 tablespoon*], a few young onions [*scallions to taste*] chopped small, a little salt, pepper, and beaten mace; beat up twelve or fourteen eggs very well [*6 to 7*], and mix all together; set a stew-pan over the stove; put in a quarter of a pound [*2 tablespoons*] of butter to melt, and break a quarter of a pound more [*2 tablespoons*] into your aumlet: When your butter is hot, pour the aumlet in, and with a knife job it [*poke it*], to let your butter down by degrees; fry it of a pale brown on both sides: Send it to table, garnished with Seville orange in quarters. Thus you may do musclse, cockles, or oysters. These are pretty dishes for Lent, or fast days.

This recipe is the first one we include from *The Modern Art of Cookery*, an eighteenth-century English cookbook that is part of the museum's Chellis collection of rare books. As with the French egg recipes, we found this recipe needs very few changes to make it as delicious now as it was when the book was published. We have added updated recommendations, and suggest using a large omelette pan, or dividing the mixture to cook omelettes in individual serving sizes in a smaller pan.

One of the premier chefs in the Southeast was born and raised in Alabama. After international training at some of the world's finest restaurants, Frank Stitt returned to Alabama and, along with his wife, Frances, opened three of the Southeast's finest restaurants. This recipe, from Highlands Bar and Grill, is a wonderful example of Frank's philosophy about cooking. It combines classical techniques with regional ingredients and traditions, and is, indeed, a culinary masterpiece.

❧ GRITS WITH WILD MUSHROOMS, THYME, AND COUNTRY HAM

Serves 4

4 cups water
Salt
1 cup stone ground yellow grits
1 egg
2 tablespoons butter
Freshly ground white pepper
4 tablespoons good Parmesan cheese (Parmigiano-Reggiano is best)

- Bring water to a boil with salt.
- Slowly stir in grits; continue stirring, with a large wooden spoon, until thickened, about 12 minutes.
- Pour into large bowl; add butter, pepper, and Parmesan.
- Whip until ingredients are combined. Add eggs and stir thoroughly.
- Place in buttered 4– to 6–ounce ramekins and bake in water bath at 325° for 20 minutes. Remove from oven and keep warm.
- Unmold grits onto warm plates. Ladle sauce around grits, and surround with mushrooms and ham. Garnish with thyme.

Sauce
1/2 cup white wine
2 tablespoons white wine vinegar
2 shallots, finely chopped
1 bay leaf
Scraps from country ham
1 dried red hot pepper
1 tablespoon cream
1/2 pound unsalted butter, cut into cubes
2 tablespoons Parmesan
Salt and pepper to taste
Lemon juice to taste

- Reduce wine, vinegar, shallots, red pepper, and country ham until 1 tablespoon liquid remains.
- Add cream and stir over low heat.
- Whisk in butter until all absorbed. Strain.
- Add 2 tablespoons Parmesan; season to taste with salt, pepper, and lemon juice.
- Reserve in warm place.

Ham

2 thin slices country ham, cut into julienne (thin strips)

1/2 pound mushrooms (chanterelles, morels, shitakes, or oyster mushrooms) cut into thick slices

1 shallot, minced

1 clove garlic, minced

1 tablespoon olive oil

- Sauté ham, mushrooms, shallot, and garlic in olive oil until just done, about 3 minutes.

∾ COUNTRY GRITS AND SAUSAGE

Serves 8

2 cups water

1/2 teaspoon salt

1/2 cup uncooked quick grits

4 cups [16 ounces] shredded extra-sharp Cheddar cheese

4 eggs, beaten

1 cup milk

1/2 teaspoon dried whole thyme

1/8 teaspoon garlic powder

Pinch celery salt

2 pounds mild sausage

- Bring water and salt to a boil, and stir in grits.
- Return to boil, reduce heat, and cook for 4 minutes, stirring occasionally.
- Combine grits and cheese in a large mixing bowl, stirring until cheese melts.
- Combine eggs, milk, thyme, garlic powder, and celery salt; mix well.
- Add a small amount of grits to mixture, stirring well.
- Stir egg mixture into remaining grits mixture.
- Add cooked, crumbled, and drained sausage, stirring well.
- Pour into a 12 x 8 x 2–inch baking dish; cover and refrigerate overnight.
- Remove dish from refrigerator and let it stand for 15 minutes.
- Bake, covered, at 350° for 50 to 55 minutes.
- Garnish with tomato roses and parsley.

This recipe can be halved and baked in a 9 x 13–inch dish for 45 minutes.

65

The Lakeview district of Birmingham's historical Southside is fast becoming a mecca of fine restaurants, trendy night spots, and up-and-coming art-related businesses. One of the first restaurants to open in the area was Bombay Café, and it has continued to be one of the city's most popular and beautiful restaurants. The innovative recipe offered here is an example of why the Bombay ranks among Birmingham's best.

 ## BOMBAY CORNMEAL AND LUMP CRABMEAT PANCAKES

Makes 16 to 18 pancakes, serves 8

1 cup self-rising cornmeal
1/2 cup all-purpose flour
Pinch of baking powder
2 tablespoons light brown sugar
Pinch of salt, black pepper, and garlic powder
2 extra large eggs
1 cup buttermilk
1/2 cup heavy cream
2 tablespoons white Zinfandel wine
2 tablespoons melted butter
1/2 pound jumbo lump crabmeat
2 tablespoons chopped fresh chives
Balsamic vinegar and sour cream for topping

- Sift all dry ingredients into a stainless steel mixing bowl.
- In a separate bowl, blend together eggs, buttermilk, cream, wine, and melted butter.
- Whip this mixture into dry ingredients.
- Stir in crabmeat and chives.
- Let stand 15 to 20 minutes.
- Pour batter onto griddle into 6–inch pancakes, and cook until golden brown on each side.
- Serve pancakes with balsamic vinegar and sour cream.

 ## PANZEROTTI

Serves 6 as a main dish, 36 as an appetizer

Classic Crepes
2 eggs
2 tablespoons melted butter or salad oil
1 1/3 cups milk
1 cup all-purpose flour
1/2 teaspoon salt

- Place ingredients in a blender in the order listed.
- Cover and blend at high speed for 20 to 30 seconds.
- Scrape down the sides of the container and blend a few more seconds.
- The crepe batter should be thin enough to run freely around the bottom of a 6–inch crepe pan when it is tilted.
- Use non-stick spray to cook the crepes.
- Cook each approximately 1 minute on each side.
- Makes 14 to 16 [6–inch] crepes.

Filling

2 eggs, beaten
2 cups ricotta cheese
1 1/2 cups grated Swiss cheese
1 [10–ounce] package chopped spinach, squeezed dry
1 1/2 cups bread crumbs
1/2 cup Parmesan cheese
1/4 teaspoon pepper
Dash garlic powder

- Combine eggs, ricotta, Swiss cheese, spinach, bread crumbs, Parmesan, pepper, and garlic powder. Mix well.
- Spoon 1/2 cup of filling in the center of each crepe.
- Roll up, cut in thirds, and fill two 8–inch round baking pans with the rolls.

Sauce

1/2 cup butter
1 cup cream
1/2 cup Parmesan cheese

- Melt butter; add cream and Parmesan and cook until slightly thickened.

- Pour sauce over filled crepes.
- Bake in two 8–inch baking dishes at 400° for 45 minutes.

Making the crepes is a little involved, but the results of this dish are spectacular and more than worth the effort!

Our second entry from *The Modern Art of Cookery* is a selection of eighteenth-century pancake recipes. Once again we have included contemporary measurements and instructions. We offer three recipes that are unusual and fulfill a variety of needs. The first, for basic pancakes, while not as simple as pouring out premade batter, has a unique taste that will make this recipe a change from the ordinary. The second, Scotch Pancakes, comes close to our contemporary crepes recipes. The original recipe makes a sweet dish to be used as part of a breakfast buffet or dessert; they are delicious spread with jam or jelly and rolled or folded in quarters. It is also a good recipe for luncheon crepes to be filled with creamed seafood, chicken, or ham filling, or any other savory filling. The recipe for fine pancakes is definitely for a dessert or sweet brunch dish, perhaps served with a topping of fruit and/or whipped cream. We have cut the first two recipes in half in our notes, and also lessened the amount of sherry used. We tested using cream; if you use milk, you may have to increase the amount of flour slightly. If you are cooking for hungry appetites, just double the ingredient amounts.

 **TO MAKE PANCAKES**

Makes 8 to 10 4–inch pancakes

Take nine eggs, and half the whites [*1 whole egg plus 2 yolks*], a quart of cream [*2 cups*], and half a pound of fresh butter melted [*1/2 cup*], beat the eggs with it, warm the cream, and mix it all together, with a glass of sack [*1/4 cup sherry*], a little beaten cinnamon [*1/2 teaspoon*], and sage [*optional, 1/8 teaspoon if using it*], and flour sufficient to make it into a batter [*2 to 2 1/2 cups*]. Put a pan over the stove to be hot, then pour in the batter of what thickness you please, and fry them without any butter. [*We suggest using a non-stick pan.*]

TO MAKE SCOTCH PANCAKES

Makes 10 to 12 7–inch crepes

To a pint of cream [*1 cup*] beat up eight eggs, leaving out two whites [*1 whole egg plus 2 yolks*], a quarter of a pound [*1/4 cup*] of butter melted, one spoonful of flour [*3/4 to 1 cup for a thin batter*], a nutmeg grated [*1 teaspoon*], three spoonfuls of sack [*1/4 cup sherry*], and a little sugar [*2 tablespoons*]. When the butter is cool mix all together into a batter; have ready a stove with charcoal, and a small frying-pan no bigger than a plate, tye a piece of butter in a clean cloth; when the pan is hot rub this round it [*or use cooking spray*], and put in the batter with a spoon, run it round the pan very thin and fry them only on one side; put a saucer into the middle of the dish, and lay the pancakes over it, till it is like a little pyramid; strew pounded sugar between every pancake, and garnish the dish with Seville oranges cut in small quarters. [*We recommend any fruit that is good with pancakes.*]

TO MAKE FINE PANCAKES

Makes 10 to 12 4–inch pancakes

Take half a pint of cream [*1 cup*], half a pint of sack [*1/2 cup sherry*], the yolks of sixteen eggs well beaten and strained [*10 yolks*], a little salt, half a pound of sugar pounded [*1/2 cup*], a little beaten cinnamon, mace and nutmeg [*1/4 teaspoon each*]; then put in as much flour as will make it into a thin batter [*about 2 cups*], and fry it in fresh butter; this sort of pancakes will not be crisp.

SEAFOOD

(Page 69) Wayne Thiebaud (American, born 1920), *Fish Circle*, 1975. Oil on canvas, 16 1/4 x 20 inches. Museum purchase with funds partially provided by the National Endowment for the Arts, a federal agency, and the Birmingham Art Association, in memory of Mr. and Mrs. Joseph Simpson.

Starting out as a commercial artist doing sign painting, cartooning, and finally advertising art direction, Wayne Thiebaud did not turn to fine art until later in life. Because his still life paintings usually concentrate on one single subject and often include a deadpan treatment, such as the one depicted here, he is often associated with the Pop Art movement. However, his loose, painterly brush strokes and strong lighting effects, along with the use of traditional painting techniques and materials, align him more closely with traditional still life painters. The focus of his still life paintings is frequently common, unimportant, and often trivial objects, such as toys, dime-store items, or food, as depicted in *Fish Circle*.

70

SEAFOOD

੭ CAJUN POPCORN

Serves 4 to 6

1 1/2 pounds crawfish tail meat
1 small bottle Louisiana hot sauce
2 eggs, well-beaten
1 1/4 cups milk
1/2 cup corn flour or all-purpose flour
1 teaspoon sugar
1 teaspoon salt
1/2 teaspoon onion powder
1/2 teaspoon garlic powder
1/2 teaspoon white pepper
1/2 teaspoon cayenne pepper
1/8 teaspoon black pepper
1/2 teaspoon dried thyme
1/4 teaspoon dried basil
1/2 cup flour
1/2 teaspoon salt
1/4 teaspoon black pepper
1/4 teaspoon cayenne pepper
Oil for frying

- Marinate the crawfish tail meat in the hot sauce in refrigerator for at least 1 hour.
- Blend eggs and milk in a small bowl.
- In a large bowl, combine 1/2 cup corn flour, sugar, salt, garlic and onion powders, white, cayenne, and black peppers, thyme, and basil, and mix well.
- Add half the egg mixture and whisk until well-blended; then thoroughly blend in remaining egg mixture.
- Let sit at room temperature for about 20 minutes to let flour expand.
- Make seasoned flour by combining 1/2 cup flour, salt, and peppers.
- Dredge tails in seasoned flour, then coat with the batter. Fry tails, a few at a time so they do not touch in the oil, until they are a golden brown.

Large shrimp cut in thirds or tiny shrimp may be used in place of crawfish.

Cajun Popcorn is our second recipe from Dexter's on Hollywood. It again shows the strengths of our best restaurants, emphasizing contemporary Southern cooking using fresh local ingredients, this time shrimp from the Gulf. This spicy crowd pleaser is perfect for formal or informal gatherings.

71

If you like Valora Spencer's Shrimp Sherry Sauté (see next page), you will love Helen Bolvig's Cajun BBQ Shrimp. It is a "peel and eat" dish that will win raves from your guests.

❧ CAJUN B B Q SHRIMP

Serves 10 to 12

6 pounds large shrimp, unshelled
2 cups butter or margarine
3 tablespoons rosemary
1 1/2 tablespoons salt
1 1/2 tablespoons pepper
1 1/2 teaspoons cayenne pepper
1 1/2 teaspoons garlic juice
6 cloves garlic, crushed
1 teaspoon oregano
1/2 cup dry white wine

- Clean shrimp, leaving shells on. Place in a covered container and refrigerate.
- Melt butter in a sauce pan; add seasonings and wine. Let the mixture cool.
- Pour mixture over shrimp, cover, and marinate in refrigerator for at least 4 hours.
- Place shrimp and marinade in a large baking dish. Bake for 30 minutes at 350°. Stir several times, checking for doneness after 20 minutes.

This is a "peel and eat" dish that needs only a green salad and French bread.

❧ SHRIMP SEACREST

Serves 6

1/4 cup chopped green onions
2 teaspoons minced garlic
1 cup melted butter or margarine
2 pounds large shrimp, peeled and deveined
1 teaspoon lemon juice
1 tablespoon white wine
1/2 teaspoon salt
Coarsely ground black pepper to taste
1 teaspoon dried dill weed
1 teaspoon chopped fresh parsley
3 French rolls, split lengthwise and toasted

- In a large skillet, sauté onions and garlic in butter until onions are tender.
- Add shrimp, lemon juice, white wine, salt, and pepper. Cook over medium heat for approximately 5 minutes, stirring frequently.
- Add dill weed and parsley.
- Spoon mixture over toasted French rolls and serve immediately.

❧ TEQUILA SHRIMP

Serves 4

1/4 cup olive oil
1/4 cup quality Tequila
2 tablespoons red wine vinegar
1/4 cup lime juice
1 tablespoon crushed red pepper (not cayenne)
1/2 teaspoon salt
2 cloves garlic, pressed
1 medium red bell pepper, cut into narrow strips
1 medium green bell pepper, cut into narrow strips
1 medium red onion, cut into narrow wedges
24 large raw shrimp, peeled and deveined, tail intact

- Mix all ingredients together except vegetables and shrimp. Pour into a shallow plastic or glass dish. Stir in shrimp, covering with marinade. Lay vegetables on top and cover with plastic wrap.
- Let mixture marinate in refrigerator for approximately 4 hours.
- Thread shrimp onto skewers and grill, using marinade to baste shrimp while grilling.
- Sauté vegetables in remaining marinade and serve with shrimp.

❧ SHRIMP SHERRY SAUTÉ

Serves 4 to 6

2 1/2 pounds fresh or frozen shrimp, uncooked
1/2 cup margarine
1 clove garlic
3 tablespoons minced parsley
1/2 cup cooking sherry

- Peel and devein fresh shrimp. If frozen shrimp is used, it should be thawed before cooking.
- Melt margarine in a large skillet. Add garlic and cook for 2 minutes; remove garlic. Add shrimp and sauté over medium heat until shrimp turns pink.
- Stir in parsley and sherry and cook for 30 seconds.

Excellent with rice and a spinach salad.

This is a special recipe for special people, submitted by Valora H. Spencer. It is a fast and easy introductory taste of New Orleans Creole cooking. Bon Appetit!

73

∽ FIRECRACKER SHRIMP

Serves 4

1 teaspoon cayenne pepper
1/4 teaspoon dried oregano
1/2 teaspoon dried rosemary
1/2 teaspoon crushed red peppers
1 teaspoon fresh cracked black pepper
1/2 teaspoon salt
1 1/2 teaspoons minced garlic
1/4 cup margarine
1/4 cup olive oil
1 teaspoon Worcestershire sauce
1 pound large shrimp, heads removed and discarded
1/4 cup thinly sliced green onion tops

- Mix cayenne, oregano, rosemary, red pepper, black pepper, salt, and garlic.
- Melt margarine in olive oil over medium heat. Add seasoning mixture and Worcestershire sauce. Simmer 2 minutes, whisking constantly.
- Add shrimp and onion tops. Sauté until shrimp turn pink and opaque, approximately 3 to 4 minutes.
- Serve in individual dishes with a mound of rice in the center, and sautéed vegetables on the side.

❧ REGAL RIETTA SHRIMP

Serves 10

3 pounds shrimp, cleaned and cooked
1 1/2 cups mayonnaise
1 cup finely chopped celery
1/2 cup finely chopped onion
1/2 teaspoon salt
2 tablespoons Worcestershire sauce
4 hard cooked eggs, chopped
2 tablespoons pimento, chopped
2 cloves garlic, chopped
1 [8–ounce] can sliced water chestnuts
1 [10 1/2–ounce] can condensed cream of mushroom soup
1 cup sour cream
Paprika

- Mix all the ingredients together, and pour into a 9 x 13–inch casserole.
  Sprinkle top with paprika.
- Bake at 350° for 30 minutes, or until bubbly.

Excellent served over rice, with broiled tomatoes, green salad, and rolls.

This recipe was given to us by Ethel Howard, widow of the museum's first director, Richard Howard. This lovely casserole was presented to the Howards one evening at their condo in Gulf Shores, Alabama, by George Rietta, mother of Birmingham's late sculptor, John Rietta. Ethel made a few minor changes in the recipe but named it after Mrs. Rietta. Served with broiled tomatoes and a green salad, it makes a great company dish.

Seafood has always been a favorite food in Birmingham, and as we already mentioned, one of the best places in Birmingham to get seafood is the Cabana Café. In this recipe, fresh vegetables and shrimp are mixed with pasta to make an easy, light, and scrumptious summer meal.

∾ GARLIC SHRIMP AND ANGEL HAIR PASTA

Serves 2

12 small shrimp
1/2 cup chablis or other dry white wine
1/2 cup diced tomatoes
1/2 cup diced green onions
1 cup garlic butter (recipe follows)
8 ounces angel hair pasta

- Cook pasta according to package directions until al denté. Drain and keep warm.
- Braise shrimp in chablis 3 to 5 minutes.
- Add tomato and onions, and cook an additional 2 minutes. Drain off excess liquid.
- Add garlic butter and sauté until butter melts. Shrimp should be pink.
- Put pasta in a serving bowl. Pour shrimp mixture over pasta and serve.

Garlic butter

1 cup butter
1 1/2 tablespoons minced garlic
1 1/2 tablespoons parsley flakes
1/4 tablespoon Old Bay seasoning

- Mix all ingredients together in a blender.

∾ SHRIMP AND CHEESE CASSEROLE

Serves 6

1/4 pound fresh mushrooms
2 tablespoons butter
1 pound fresh cooked and shelled shrimp
1 1/2 cups cooked white rice
1 1/2 cups [6 ounces] grated Cheddar cheese
1/2 cup cream
3 tablespoons ketchup
1/2 teaspoon Worcestershire sauce
1/2 teaspoon salt
Dash pepper

- Slice mushrooms and sauté slowly in butter for 10 minutes.
- Mix mushrooms and juice gently with shrimp, rice, and cheese in a 4–quart casserole.
- Combine cream, ketchup, Worcestershire sauce, and seasonings; mix well and add to shrimp mixture.
- Cover casserole and bake at 350° for 25 minutes.

❧ SHRIMP PARMESAN

Serves 4

2 bunches of green onions, chopped
1 clove garlic, pressed
1/2 cup butter or margarine
Juice of 1 lemon
1 tablespoon Worcestershire sauce
Dash of ground red pepper (optional)
2 pounds raw shrimp, peeled and deveined
1 [7–ounce] package vermicelli
1/2 cup grated Parmesan cheese
2 tablespoons chopped fresh parsley

- In a large skillet, sauté onions and garlic in butter for about 5 minutes. Add lemon juice and Worcestershire sauce.
- Add red pepper and shrimp, cover, and cook at medium temperature until shrimp is done, approximately 10 minutes.
- Prepare pasta according to package directions; drain well. Mix with Parmesan cheese and parsley.
- Pour shrimp sauce over pasta and serve.

Good with fresh spinach salad and hot French bread.

Vincent's Market recently enlarged and renovated their store, offering more space for dining in a sunny, plant-filled restaurant. Shrimp and Pesto is one of the tantalizing selections that can be purchased for in-house dining or carry out. Either way, it offers a delicious, no-hassle solution to calm a hectic day.

The first of two seafood dishes from *The Modern Art of Cookery* is a fascinating eighteenth-century English dish for lobster pie. The English learned early that it is convenient and tasty to put ingredients in a crust and bake them, thereby eliminating the need for tableware. We have updated this recipe, and found, in testing, that it is also delicious using a variety of shellfish, such as shrimp and scallops, or whitefish, such as sole or flounder, or especially a salmon filling. The lobster can simply be substituted with medium-sized pieces of these other seafoods.

We have also included a recipe for puff pastry, from *The Modern Art of Cookery* that is rich and delicious. We have halved it to make one double-crust pie, and put 1-crust measurements in parentheses. Puff paste is difficult to work with, and must be kneaded 10 to 15 minutes for elasticity before incorporating the extra butter. It is possible to add all the butter at once for a delicious, yet not so difficult, crust.

❧ SHRIMP AND PESTO ALFREDO

Serves 4

24 medium shrimp, peeled and deveined
12 ounces fusilli
3 cups cream
4 tablespoons basil pesto
1/4 cup Parmesan cheese
1/4 cup minced garlic
Black pepper and salt to taste

- Cook fusilli al denté. Drain and rinse with cold water to stop cooking.
- In sauce pan, combine shrimp, garlic, basil pesto, and cream. Simmer until shrimp are cooked and cream is reduced by about 1/4.
- Add cooked fusilli, Parmesan cheese, and black pepper.
- Heat until pesto is hot, season to taste.

❧ TO MAKE A LOBSTER PYE

Sheet your dish with puff-paste [*recipe follows*], then take two boiled lobsters, and cut the tails into eight pieces; take the meat out of the claws, and lay the tails and claws into the pye [*about 2 pounds lobster meat cut in bite size pieces*]; pick out all the meat from the chimes, and bruise the bodies very fine; melt half a pound of butter [*1 cup*], put the picked meat and bodies into it, with two spoonfuls of grated bread [*1/2 cup fresh bread crumbs*], and a glass of white wine [*1/2 cup*]; season it with pepper, salt, and nutmeg [*to taste*]; pour this over the lobsters, lay on the lid, and bake it in a slow oven [*325° for 45 minutes*].

❧ TO MAKE A PUFF PASTE FOR VENISON, OR OTHER PIES

Take a pound of butter [*2/3 (1/2) cup*], and a pound of flour [*2 (1 1/2) cups*], pinch a quarter of a pound into the flour first [*1/3 (1/4) cup*], mix it with water not too stiff [*6 (4) tablespoons or so, and knead for 10 to 15 minutes*], and roll it out pretty thin; then pinch another layer of the butter, about the bigness of a half a crown, in thin pieces, and lay it upon your paste [*using half of the remaining butter*]; fold the paste up, put no flour upon your butter, and as little as you can in rolling of it out upon your dresser; then roll it out again, pinch in the remainder of the butter, [*fold it over*] and roll it once more. In the summer time, make it in a cool place, or early in the morning. [*We recommend chilling the dough before rolling it out, especially if the butter is not layered, but put in at one time.*]

❧ CRAB ELEGANTE

Serves 10

2 cups thick white sauce (recipe follows)
1 teaspoon Worcestershire sauce
1/8 teaspoon white pepper
3/4 teaspoon salt
1 green pepper, minced
1 medium onion, minced
1 clove garlic, crushed
1/4 cup butter, divided
1 1/2 cups [6 ounces] sliced fresh mushrooms
1 pound fresh lump crab meat
1/4 cup chopped parsley
1 lemon, cut into six slices

• Stir Worcestershire sauce, pepper, and salt into white sauce.
• Sauté green pepper, onion, and garlic in 2 tablespoons of the butter for 5 minutes; add to white sauce.
• Sauté mushrooms in remaining 2 tablespoons of butter and add to white sauce.
• Fold in crab meat and parsley.
• Pile mixture into 6 buttered seafood shells or ramekins. Top each with a lemon slice, and sprinkle with paprika.
• Bake for 30 minutes at 350°, or until bubbly.

White Sauce

1/4 cup butter or margarine
1/4 cup all-purpose flour
2 cups milk
3 tablespoons heavy cream

• Melt butter in a 3–quart saucepan, being careful not to burn.
• Slowly stir in flour, using a wire whisk, until mixture is thoroughly blended.
• Add milk, stirring constantly with wire whisk.
• When mixture is thick and smooth, stir in cream.

79

This is the recipe for one of Birmingham's all-time favorite dishes. Thursday is Crab Cakes day at Highlands Bar and Grill, and the fans are legion. For those who will take the time and effort to make this at home, you will be justly rewarded as you serve this dish. We are sure, however, that if giving you this recipe has any impact on the number of diners lining up for Thursday lunches at Highlands, we guarantee the numbers will only increase.

❧ CRAB CAKES

Serves 4

2 pounds fresh blue crab meat
3 cups fresh bread crumbs
6 tablespoons butter, melted and cooled
2 eggs, beaten
2 tablespoons chopped shallots
1 tablespoon chopped green onions
2 tablespoons chopped parsley
2 tablespoons lemon juice
Pinch freshly grated nutmeg
Pinch cayenne
Salt and pepper to taste
2 eggs, beaten with 2 tablespoons water
1 cup fresh bread crumbs
3 tablespoons clarified butter or butter with a few drops of peanut oil added
Lemon wedges for garnish

- Combine crab meat, 3 cups breadcrumbs, butter, eggs, shallots, onion, parsley, lemon juice, nutmeg, salt, pepper, and cayenne. Toss to combine. Taste and adjust seasonings.
- Form 8 patties, being sure not to press too firmly.
- Dip in egg wash, then 1 cup breadcrumbs (day old French or Italian bread). Let rest on a rack for a few minutes.
- Heat clarified butter until almost to smoking point.
- Add crabcakes; do not crowd.
- Cook until golden, about 3 to 4 minutes. Turn and cook until just done.
- Remove from pan and keep warm until ready to serve.
- Place crab cakes on warm plate, surround with buerre blanc, and garnish with lemon wedges.

Buerre Blanc

1 cup white wine
1/4 cup white wine vinegar
2 tablespoons chopped shallots
1 tablespoon cream
1 cup butter
Lemon juice, salt and pepper to taste

- Combine wine, vinegar, and shallots. Heat and reduce to a syrupy glaze.
- Remove pan from heat; stir in cream. Reduce.
- Over low heat, begin to add butter bit by bit until it is thoroughly incorporated.
- Add salt, pepper, and lemon juice; strain.
- Hold at warm room temperature until needed.

❧ CRAB AND SPINACH CASSEROLE

Serves 8

1/4 cup butter or margarine
1/4 cup onion, chopped
2 [10 1/2–ounce] cans condensed cream of mushroom soup
1 [6–ounce] can sliced mushrooms
1 cup sour cream
1/2 cup grated Parmesan cheese
1/2 teaspoon dry mustard
1 tablespoon chopped parsley or chives
1 pound crab meat
2 [10–ounce] packages frozen chopped spinach
Paprika

- In a large skillet, melt butter or margarine and sauté the onion.
- Add soup, mushrooms, sour cream, cheese, mustard, and parsley.
  Simmer until smooth.
- Stir in crab meat.
- Cook frozen spinach according to package directions. Drain well.
- In a 2–quart casserole, layer spinach and crab mixture; sprinkle with paprika.
- Bake 20 to 30 minutes at 350°.
- Serve over cooked rice.

A close neighbor of the museum is the newly-opened Sheraton Civic Center. Their Atrium restaurant is a prime spot for an early or late dinner in the heart of the city. And their recipe for scallops baked in pesto and wine, served with angel hair pasta and tomatoes, is a light and simple dish packed with flavor, and suitable for a light dinner or luncheon entrée.

 SCALLOPS IN PESTO

Serves 4

1 cup olive oil
2 cups fresh basil torn into small pieces
1 tablespoon pine nuts or walnuts
2 tablespoons chopped garlic
2 tablespoons fresh grated Romano cheese
1/2 tablespoon fresh cracked pepper
1/2 tablespoon salt
1 1/4 pounds fresh scallops
1/2 cup chablis or chardonnay
Salt and pepper to taste
10 ounces angel hair pasta
2 tomatoes, diced
1/4 cup olive oil
Salt and pepper to taste

- Combine 1 cup olive oil, basil, pine nuts or walnuts, garlic, Romano cheese, pepper and salt in a blender and purée thoroughly to make pesto.
- Using approximately 5 ounces of scallops per person, place scallops in an oven-proof dish and sprinkle with salt and pepper.
- Add wine and all but 2 tablespoons of pesto.
- Place under broiler, and broil for 5 minutes.
- Remove from heat.
- Turn scallops, and brush with remaining pesto. Return to broiler for an additional 5 minutes.
- Cook pasta according to package directions, to al denté. Drain and rinse lightly.
- Toss pasta with diced tomatoes and olive oil and salt and pepper to taste.

⌒ SCALLOPS WITH SHALLOT BUTTER SAUCE

Serves 4 to 6

1 pound sea scallops
3/4 cup butter
3 tablespoons finely chopped shallots
Salt to taste
1 tablespoon lemon juice
2 tablespoons chopped parsley
1/3 cup finely ground fresh bread crumbs
2 tablespoons pine nuts

- Rinse and dry scallops.
- Place in ramekins or baking shells.
- In a food processor, mix butter, shallots, salt, lemon juice, parsley, and bread crumbs. Be sure mixture is not too fine.
- Stir in pine nuts.
- Place equal amounts of mixture on top of scallops. Bake at 375° for 10 minutes, or until hot and bubbly.

⌒ GRILLED SCALLOPS EN BROCHETTE

Serves 4

1 pound fresh scallops
8 strips bacon
3 tablespoons melted butter
1/2 teaspoon salt
1/8 teaspoon freshly ground pepper
Lemon wedges

- Wash scallops and dry thoroughly.
- In a frying pan, cook bacon partially, so it begins to brown but is still soft.
- On 4 skewers, loosely intertwine bacon strips and scallops. Brush with melted butter and sprinkle with salt and pepper.
- Grill over hot coals or broil 3 to 5 inches from heat for 5 to 10 minutes, turning once.
- Serve with lemon wedges.

Several years ago the Tutwiler Hotel was restored and reopened as the premier downtown hotel. The dining is superb, featuring weekend brunches and classic evening fare with a contemporary twist. The recipe they contributed exemplifies this attitude. They have taken a Southwestern favorite, the taco, and updated it with a unique combination of fresh seafood and an unusual salsa. The result is delightful.

❧ SEAFOOD TACO WITH GRAPEFRUIT SALSA

Serves 4

2 tablespoons butter
16 to 20 shrimp [1/2 pound] cleaned, shelled, and deveined
1/2 pound sea scallops
1/2 pound Canadian snow crabmeat (leg portions)
Small red onion
1/4 pound Shitake mushrooms, julienned
1 small Jalapeño
1 finely diced pepper
12 pitted black olives, diced
12 pitted green olives, diced
1/4 cup white wine
1/2 cup heavy cream
1/4 cup sweet cream
Salt and pepper to taste
4 6–inch soft taco shells
Grapefruit salsa (recipe follows)

- In a large skillet sauté 2 tablespoons butter on medium-high heat. When butter begins to bubble, add shrimp and scallops.
- Sauté for 1 1/2 minutes.
- Add snow crab legs, sauté for an additional minute.
- Add onions, mushrooms, jalapeño pepper, green pepper, and olives. Sauté for 1 1/2 minutes or until the mixture loses approximately 1/3 of its moisture.
- Add white wine and reduce mixture by 1/3. Add heavy cream.
- Reduce mixture by 1/3, and add sweet cream and salt and pepper to taste.
- Reduce heat. Cook, stirring until mixture is well blended.
- Divide mixture equally into taco shells and roll.

Salsa
Grapefruit segments from 2 fresh grapefruits
1/4 cup sour cream
Juice of 1/2 lemon
1 tomato, peeled, seeded, and diced
1/2 ounce chopped cilantro

- Gently mix all ingredients except cilantro, in a bowl.
- Spread the grapefruit salsa equally across the rolled tacos, and sprinkle with cilantro.
- Serve immediately.

Have all ingredients ready before beginning to cook. To keep your product crisp and not soggy, the temperature of the stove should always be on high, since as the new ingredients are placed into the pan, they will reduce the temperature.

❧ SEAFOOD EN CASSEROLE

Serves 10

3/4 cup uncooked rice
1 [6–ounce] can fancy crabmeat
1 [6–ounce] can claw crabmeat
2 [5–ounce] cans shrimp
1 medium green pepper, finely chopped
1 medium onion, finely chopped
1 cup finely chopped celery
1/2 teaspoon salt
Red and black pepper to taste
1 tablespoon Worcestershire sauce
1 cup mayonnaise
1 cup sour cream
Fresh bread crumbs to taste
Paprika to taste
Parsley for garnish

- Cook rice according to package directions.
- Mix all ingredients, except the last three, and pour into a 2–quart casserole. Sprinkle with fresh bread crumbs and paprika.
- Bake for 30 minutes at 350°.
- Garnish with parsley.

Serve with tossed salad and French bread.
Fresh seafood may be substituted, but use of canned seafood makes this a convenient and fast dish.

Anthony's is located on Seventh Avenue South in an area that has been home to a number of excellent Birmingham restaurants. They have a faithful following since they offer the finest in ethnic food, Italian, Greek, and Jewish among others, as well as atmosphere. They also take advantage of local fresh ingredients and feature a number of delicious seafood dishes, including the recipe shown here. This unusual and delectable dish combines artichokes and oysters to make Italian like you've never tasted before.

❧ ARTICHOKE CASTROVILLE-OYSTER CASSEROLE

Serves 4

4 large artichoke hearts
1/2 cup butter, divided
1/4 cup all-purpose flour
2 tablespoons green onion
3/4 teaspoon salt
3/4 teaspoon pepper
3/4 teaspoon thyme
3 dozen oysters and oyster liquid
1/4 cup sherry
1 cup Italian bread crumbs
1/4 cup Parmesan cheese

- Boil artichoke hearts until tender. Drain and mash.
- Melt 1/4 cup butter and stir in flour with a wire whisk to make a roux; cook, stirring, until the mixture is a golden brown, being careful not to burn.
- Cook onions in oyster liquid with seasonings and mashed artichoke hearts.
- Sauté oysters in remaining 1/4 cup butter until the edges curl.
- Mix the roux, onion, artichoke mixture, and oysters together, and let it cook for approximately 10 to 12 minutes on very low heat.
- Stir in sherry and place in casserole dish. Top with bread crumbs.
- Bake at 400° for 10 to 12 minutes.

86

Our second eighteenth-century English seafood recipe from *The Modern Art of Cookery* is so timeless and luscious we have had to add almost no additional instructions to the original recipe. When testing, we found the recipe will fit four to six French rolls, depending on their size. If you want crunchy rolls, it is not necessary to put them "into the stew pan, and just turn them round." It is also delicious when made with shrimp or scallops. And if there is not enough fish "liquor" to cook them in, add a little fish stock or clam juice, 1/4 to 1/2 cup should do the trick. Canned oysters work fine, also.

❧ TO MAKE OYSTER LOAVES

Take a French roll [*1 roll per serving*], cut a hole in the top, take out all the crumb as clean as you can, but be careful you do not break through the sides; take a pint of oysters, put them into a saucepan with a blade of mace, a bit of onion, and some whole pepper, when they are stewed enough, take them out, and wash them very clean in their own liquor; strain the liquor into a clean sauce pan, add to it a spoonful of ketchup [*2 tablespoons*], and about a gill [*1/2 cup*] of red wine; burn some butter [*2 tablespoons*], and thicken it with flour [*2 tablespoons*] till it is of a fine brown, and very thick [*see roux instructions in recipe above for procedure*]; put in the oysters and liquor, toss them up together, then put your loaves into the stew pan, and just turn them round, fill your loaves with the oysters and sauce, put on the tops, and send them to table, it is a pretty side dish for a first coarse.

You may either harden your rolls before the fire, or fry them of a fine brown which you like the best, before you fill them.

❧ TO BROIL SALMON

Cut fresh salmon into pieces, about an inch thick, strew some pepper and salt, and a little dust of flour over them; butter some writing paper, make it up in the form of dripping-pans, and pin the corners; lay in the slices of salmon into the paper-pans, and broil them a fine brown, over a clear fire. If you find the paper is like to catch, put in a little bit of butter, and that will prevent it: When the salmon is done, take it out of the papers, lay it into a warm dish, with melted butter in a cup.

We included this *Modern Art of Cookery* recipe because we found it to be enchanting, the thought of little parchment paper pans over a clear fire. The cooking instructions, minus the paper-pans, will work just as well today if you are grilling your salmon.

❧ BLUE MARLIN MOSCOWIT

Serves 4

2 pounds blue marlin fillets
2 tablespoons olive oil
2 tablespoons butter
1/3 cup chopped onion
1/3 cup chopped parsley
6 ounces fresh asparagus
Juice of one lemon
1/3 cup white wine
1/3 cup sour cream
1 cup vodka
Caviar to garnish

- Pan fry fish in olive oil until almost done, 3 to 5 minutes on each side. Remove to serving platter.
- In the same pan, melt butter and add onion, asparagus, parsley, and lemon juice. Sauté until asparagus is tender and remove it to serving platter.
- Add white wine, cook until liquid is reduced to half.
- Add sour cream and vodka and heat through, but do not boil.

To serve, arrange fish and asparagus on heated serving platter; pour sauce over it and garnish with red and black caviar.

Buttiker's Cafe is well known for its catering and fine dining, and is located in Crestline Village. Chef Otto Buttiker is originally from Austria, but has adapted his classical training to suit the tastes and ingredients of the deep South. He has very generously contributed four recipes that are all fast, contemporary, and absolutely scrumptious. The first two are for pan-fried fish with quick and easy sauces made in the same pan used to cook the fish. The recipes given will serve four, but the amount of fish can be cut down to serve two (6 to 8 ounces per person for the blue marlin, 8 to 10 ounces per person for the amberjack). Use of the freshest ingredients will assure a gourmet delight.

87

88

Eugène Boudin (French, 1824–98),
Harbor at Larmont, 1875. Oil on canvas,
20 x 31 1/2 inches. Gift of Mr. and Mrs.
Wyatt R. Haskell in memory of Jane Porter
Nabers.

Eugène Boudin was already an established
painter by the time the impressionist
movement began to emerge. But because
he was a landscape painter and interested
in lighting effects and weather, he was
easily assimilated into the avant garde of
impressionism. A master of outdoor
painting, much of his ouvre consists of
seascapes and landscapes of Normandy
where he was born and raised. This
painting's strong visual impact comes from
the use of dynamic verticals and diagonals
set in richly-colored loose brushwork, and
a typical Boudin foil, the presence of a
red note within a canvas awash with blues
and greys.

❧ AMBERJACK MONT BLANC

Serves 2

2 pounds Amberjack
2 teaspoons olive oil
1 tablespoon butter
1/4 cup chopped green onion
1 cup white wine
1/2 cup sour cream
Salt and pepper to taste
Fresh thyme to taste
Juice of one lemon
Red lumpfish caviar, julienne green onion, or fresh chives to garnish

- Pan fry fish in olive oil until it is almost done, 3 to 5 minutes on each side. Remove and keep warm.
- Melt butter, add green onion to the pan; sauté until tender.
- Deglaze the pan with white wine.
- Reduce wine to half, then add sour cream.
- Heat through and season with pepper, salt, fresh thyme, and lemon juice.
- Return Amberjack to the sauce and heat through.

Serve fish on a warm plate or platter. Pour sauce over and garnish with red lumpfish caviar and fresh cut green onion or chives.

Established in 1912, The Bright Star holds the distinction of being one of the oldest and most consistently popular restaurants in the Birmingham area. Located in Bessemer, it has been satisfying diners for over eighty years. The Bright Star has always featured traditional Southern fare with a touch of Greek, and the use of the freshest ingredients guarantees delicious results. Tommy Finley, manager, and Rick Diadone, chef, have contributed the recipe for their "Famous" Greek Snapper, a quick, easy, and tasty entrée.

 ## BRIGHT STAR "FAMOUS" GREEK SNAPPER

Serves 4

1 cup all-purpose flour
1 teaspoon paprika
Juice of 4 lemons
1 cup olive oil
1 tablespoon Greek seasoning (Cavender's)
1/2 cup butter
2 pounds snapper fillets
1 tablespoon oregano

- Combine flour, paprika, and Greek seasoning in a bowl.
- Dredge snapper fillets in flour mixture.
- Melt butter in skillet or flat grill.
- Place fillets in butter in hot skillet and cook for approximately 2 minutes on each side. When snapper is done, remove from skillet and place on plates.
- Blend lemon juice, olive oil, and oregano together.
- Pour about 1/4 cup of lemon/olive oil sauce on each piece and serve.

 ## ORANGE ROUGHY PARMESAN

Serves 4

4 orange roughy fillets
1 tablespoon butter or margarine
1/2 cup regular or light mayonnaise
2 green onions, chopped
1/2 cup grated Parmesan cheese

- Arrange fish in a baking dish; dot with butter or margarine.
- Cover with plastic wrap and microwave for 4 minutes at 100 per cent power. Give dish one-quarter turn at the end of two minutes.
- Mix mayonnaise, onion, and cheese thoroughly. Spread over microwaved fish. Cover with plastic wrap, vent wrap, and microwave an additional 3 minutes on high. Give dish one-quarter turn at the end of 1 1/2 minutes.
- Let stand for 5 minutes before serving.

∽ TROUT STUFFED WITH SHRIMP AND CRABMEAT

Serves 4

1 medium to large or 2 medium trout, drawn
　　(eviscerated with head and tail intact and pocket for stuffing)
1/2 pound medium shrimp, cooked til barely pink,
　　peeled, deveined, and chopped
1/2 pound crabmeat
1/2 cup seasoned fresh bread crumbs
1/2 bunch scallions, green tops only, chopped
1/2 pound fresh mushrooms, thinly sliced or chopped fine
Dry white wine

- Combine shrimp, crabmeat, bread crumbs, scallions, and mushrooms. Add only enough good dry white wine to moisten the stuffing.
- Fill trout cavity with stuffing and skewer closed with toothpicks.
- Butter heavy-duty foil and wrap trout carefully. Place on cookie sheet and bake in 400° oven or place foil-wrapped trout directly onto grill and grill over hot coals for approximately 20 minutes. If grilling, turn once halfway through cooking. Not necessary to turn if baking in oven.
- Unwrap carefully and slip onto a warmed platter. Serve with lemon garnish and dilled mayonnaise.

❧ FILLET-STUFFED TOMATOES

Serves 6

6 large tomatoes
Salt and pepper
6 thin whitefish fillets, such as sole or flounder
1 1/2 cups soft bread crumbs
2 tablespoons chopped onion
6 tablespoons minced parsley
6 tablespoons melted butter
2 tablespoons lemon juice
1 teaspoon salt
1/4 teaspoon pepper
1/2 teaspoon thyme
1/2 teaspoon savory
2 tablespoons melted butter

- Cut off tops of tomatoes and scoop centers out; salt and pepper the insides.
- Combine bread crumbs, onion, parsley, 6 tablespoons of butter, lemon juice, salt, pepper, thyme, and savory.
- Spread the mixture evenly on the 6 fillets.
- Roll up the fillets and place one in each tomato.
- Drizzle the 2 tablespoons of melted butter over the tops of the rolled fillets.
- Place stuffed tomatoes in a shallow baking dish and bake at 425° for 30 minutes.

POULTRY

(Page 93) Martha Jane Singleton Hatter Bullock (1815–1896), Quilt, c. 1861. Silk with wool challis appliqué and cotton, 66 1/2 x 65 1/2 inches. Museum purchase with partial funding provided by The Quilt Conservancy.

This quilt, made prior to 1862 by Martha Jane Hatter, is a showcase for her considerable needlework skills. The highly detailed embroidery and elaborate diamond and fish scale quilted pattern are unusual even for an elaborate quilt done during the nineteenth century. The background fabric, a chocolate brown silk taffeta, was indeed innovative in 1862, cotton being standard for appliquéd or pieced quilts at this time. Silk as a quilt fabric did not become popular until the 1880s crazy quilts. The unique combination of the central floral motif of the early nineteenth century with the background, fabrics, colors, and dimensions of Victorian decorative textiles, spans two nineteenth-century extremes in the tradition of quilting.

This quilt is one of a number made during the Civil War as part of an effort by Southern women to help raise funds for the purchase of a gunboat. A variety of fundraisers were held, including auctions where this quilt and others, as well as numerous hand-made items, were sold. These quilts soon became known as "Gunboat Quilts", and the museum is happy to have such a fine example as part of our permanent collection.

94

POULTRY

❧ POULET EN RAGOUT DANS UNE BOTEILLE
[A Ragout of Chicken In A Bottle]

Debone a chicken and carefully remove its skin. Put the skin into a bottle that does not have wicker on the outside. Some of the skin should extend outside the neck of the bottle. Prepare a forcemeat of mushrooms, truffles, sweetbreads, pigeons, egg yolks and good seasonings. With this you will stuff the boned meat of the chicken and then bend and push it into the bottle. You must then seal the mouth of the bottle with paste. You will cook this well-seasoned bottle of ragout in a marmite and remove it a little time before you plan to serve it, and let it remain simmering before the fire. And when you are ready to serve it, cut the bottle with a diamond in a way that you can remove the contents whole.

❧ CHICKEN MARINADE

Serves 10 to 14

2 cups lime juice
1 cup vegetable oil
2 cups soy sauce
3 cups red wine vinegar
4 cups diced onions
1 bunch cilantro, chopped
3 tablespoons granulated garlic
3 tablespoons chopped jalepeño peppers
1 tablespoon black pepper
1 cup water
5 pounds of chicken pieces

- Mix all ingredients together, except chicken.
- Pour marinade over chicken pieces, refrigerate, and marinate for several hours.
- Grill chicken until tender, 15 to 25 minutes, basting with marinade several times during cooking.

We have included this first poultry recipe for you entertainment rather than as a viable option to serve your guests. It comes to us from *The Delectable Past*, and was originally published in 1651 in *Le Cuisinier François*. This cookbook, by François Pierre de la Varenne, laid the foundation for classical French cuisine in the court of Louis XIV. This specific recipe was in a section dedicated to food for war. French nobles would bring their entourage of servants, including cooks, and their finest tableware to the front with them. This recipe was one that could be prepared "at the front", ensuring the nobles no inconvenience, and as little loss in quality of life as was possible. We do not recommend trying this recipe at home, but would love to have been present for the opening of the bottle.

Our first official try-this-at-home easy-and-delicious poultry recipe is from La Paz restaurant in Crestline Village. La Paz opened several years ago, and as the name implies, specializes in Southwestern cuisine. Delicious and generous food portions and great atmosphere combine to make this one of the busiest restaurants around. Their recipe is for an excellent and versatile chicken marinade we are sure you will enjoy.

95

One of the more unusual recipes we have included comes from the Sheraton Civic Center Atrium restaurant. Middle eastern in origin, Chicken Tandoori is also a healthy alternative, and was rated tops by our volunteers who sampled the recipes in this book. We hope you will enjoy it as much as we do.

❧ TANDOORI CHICKEN WITH COUSCOUS

Serves 4

5 skinless, boneless chicken breasts
1 cup non- or low-fat yogurt
1 tablespoon chopped garlic
2 tablespoons curry powder
Juice of one lime
2 tablespoons olive oil
1/2 tablespoon salt
1/4 tablespoon white pepper

- Combine yogurt, garlic, curry powder, lime juice, olive oil, salt, and pepper thoroughly.
- Place chicken in a shallow non-metallic pan and marinate in yogurt mixture overnight in refrigerator.
- Cook either under broiler or over charcoal, approximately 7 to 8 minutes on each side, or until firm.

Serve with couscous (Moroccan pasta) and tossed green salad made with cucumbers, Roma tomatoes, fresh mint, and an olive oil vinaigrette dressing.

Couscous
1/4 cup finely diced carrots
1/4 cup finely diced onions
1/4 cup finely diced celery
1 [10–ounce] package couscous
1 [16–ounce] can chicken stock
2 tablespoons butter

- Sauté carrots, onions, and celery in butter until tender, about 3 to 4 minutes.
- Add the chicken stock and butter, and bring to a boil.
- Add the couscous, stir, cover, and cook according to length of time on package directions.

～ GRILLED HAWAIIAN CHICKEN

Serves 6

Marinade
2 tablespoons toasted sesame seeds
1 tablespoon fresh ginger, grated
1/3 cup honey
1/3 cup reduced sodium soy sauce

1 fresh pineapple
6 chicken breast halves, skinned and boned
Fresh parsley and edible flowers (pansies, etc.) for garnish

- Combine marinade ingredients and set aside.
- Clean, core, and cut pineapple into 6 to 8 spears, and brush lightly with marinade. Set aside. Save some pineapple leaves for garnish.
- Trim all fat from chicken breasts. Flatten meat slightly with a wooden meat mallet and place breasts in a glass dish. Pierce meat with a fork and pour remaining marinade over breasts, turning to coat all sides. Cover with plastic wrap and refrigerate 30 minutes to 1 hour.
- Place chicken breasts on grill rack that has been sprayed with cooking spray to prevent sticking. Cook 8 to 12 minutes until chicken is tender; turn and baste often with marinade.
- Place fresh pineapple spears on grill rack and cook 5 to 7 minutes until warmed. Turn often to avoid burning.
- Serve chicken and pineapple spears arranged on serving platter and garnished with pineapple leaves, parsley, and edible flowers.

97

CHICKEN BON FEMME

Serves 6

6 large chicken breast halves, boned
1/2 cup margarine
1 medium onion, sliced
1 clove garlic, minced
2 tablespoons all-purpose flour
1/2 teaspoon salt
1/4 teaspoon pepper
1 cup chicken broth or 1 chicken bullion cube and 1 cup hot water
6 small white or red potatoes, sliced
1/2 cup red wine
Parsley

- In a large skillet (or Dutch oven), brown chicken breasts in margarine on both sides. Add onion and garlic; cook 5 minutes.
- In a small bowl, combine flour, salt, and pepper. Slowly stir in the chicken broth. Pour over browned chicken breasts.
- Cover and cook slowly until chicken is tender, approximately 25 minutes.
- Add potatoes and wine and cook until potatoes are done, approximately 20 minutes.
- Garnish with parsley.

Serve with toasted French bread and green salad.

Donna Antoon, research associate in the Painting and Sculpture department, submitted an old family recipe her mother used to make when she was a little girl. It was always a family favorite which she, in turn, made for her family after she married. Her strong feelings about the quality of this recipe were justified when she tasted chicken tarragon while traveling in France. It was almost exactly the same as her mother's old recipe. We hope you enjoy it as well. Donna recommends serving it with wild rice, green beans, and a dessert of chocolate mousse for the perfect meal.

 CHICKEN TARRAGON

Serves 4

1 chicken, split, with backbone attached
Pepper
2 tablespoons unsalted butter
2 tablespoons finely chopped shallots
2 teaspoons finely chopped fresh tarragon or 1 teaspoon dried tarragon
1/2 cup dry white wine
1/4 cup water

- Cut joint between thigh and leg to hasten cooking.
- Sprinkle chicken with pepper.
- In heavy skillet, heat butter and add chicken, skin side down.
- Cook 10 minutes or until golden brown.
- Turn, cook 5 minutes, and remove to warm plate.
- Add shallots to skillet; cook briefly.
- Add wine and tarragon and stir to dissolve particles clinging to bottom of skillet; add water.
- Return chicken to skillet, skin side up. Cover and cook for 15 minutes.
- Uncover, continue cooking, and baste frequently to glaze, about 5 minutes or until chicken is tender.
- Remove chicken to hot plate.
- Reduce sauce to half, and serve with chicken.

❧ ALMOND SHERRY CHICKEN

Serves 4

4 chicken breast halves, skinned and boned
1 teaspoon seasoned salt
1 cup all-purpose flour
1/2 cup margarine
1 medium onion, diced
1 [2 1/4–ounce] package sliced almonds
1 [4–ounce] can mushrooms, drained well
1 cup dry sherry

- Cut each breast half into 4 pieces. Combine the flour and seasoning salt. Dredge chicken pieces with flour mixture and set aside.
- In a large skillet, sauté onion in margarine.
- Add chicken and cook until it is no longer pink. Add almonds and stir well. Add mushrooms.
- Add sherry, cover, and cook slowly for 5 minutes or until liquid is reduced by one half.
- Serve with rice.

🖤 ARTICHOKE CHICKEN

Serves 8

4 large whole chicken breasts, split in half
4 tablespoons butter or margarine
1 [16–ounce] can artichokes, drained
1/2 cup chopped onion
1/3 cup all-purpose flour
1 teaspoon salt
1/4 teaspoon white pepper
1 cup chicken broth
1 cup dry white wine
1 [6–ounce] can sliced mushrooms or 8 ounces of fresh mushrooms, sliced

- In a skillet, brown chicken in butter or margarine. Transfer to a 13 x 9–inch baking dish. Arrange artichoke hearts evenly over chicken.
- Add onion to skillet and cook till it is tender.
- Combine flour and seasonings; add to onion, stirring until mixture is smooth. Stir in chicken broth and wine and cook until mixture thickens, stirring constantly.
- Add mushrooms and spoon sauce evenly over chicken.
- Bake for 45 minutes at 350°.

🖤 LEMON-LIME CHICKEN

Serves 4

2 [2 1/2–pound] broiling chickens, quartered
2 lemons
2 limes
Salt and black pepper
1 teaspoon ground ginger
1/2 teaspoon garlic powder
3 tablespoons chopped fresh parsley
1 tablespoon chopped tarragon or 1 teaspoon dried
3 tablespoons snipped dill weed
Sweet paprika
1/4 pound melted butter

- Butter a roasting pan, line with foil and butter again. Place chicken quarters, skin-side up, in pan. Sprinkle with juice of half a lemon and half a lime.
- Sprinkle herbs and seasonings, except remaining lemon and lime, over chicken in order listed. Dribble melted butter over all.
- Cover loosely with foil and bake 30 minutes at 375°. Remove foil, bake 20 minutes longer or until done. Let cool.
- Squeeze juice of half a lemon and half a lime over cooled chicken. Chill. Slice remaining lemon and lime for garnish.

❧ CHICKEN IN LEMON BUTTER SAUCE

Serves 4 to 6

2 green onions, chopped
1 [4–ounce] can mushrooms
1 [2–ounce] jar chopped pimento
1/2 cup butter or margarine
1/2 cup lemon juice
1/2 teaspoon salt, or to taste
1/4 teaspoon pepper, or to taste
1/2 teaspoon garlic powder
1 tablespoon Worcestershire sauce
4 to 6 skinless chicken breast halves

- Combine all ingredients, except chicken, in a sauce pan. Bring to a boil. Taste and correct seasonings if necessary.
- Place chicken in a 9 x 13–inch baking dish. Pour sauce over chicken.
- Bake at 350° for 1 hour and 15 minutes, or until done.
- Baste every 15 minutes.

For a more piquant sauce, increase the amount of lemon juice to 3/4 cup.

101

Our second recipe for marinated chicken comes from the Back Alley restaurant. The variation in marinade ingredients offers a tasty alternative to the La Paz recipe. The Back Alley marinade is for chicken breasts that are either baked or grilled. It is a versatile recipe which can be used for the meat portion of your meal to be served with various sauces and pasta, rice, or vegetables, and, as noted, makes a wonderful addition to a summer salad. It is one of the Back Alley's most popular dishes.

❧ MARINATED BAKED CHICKEN BREASTS
Serves 6

6 chicken breast halves, boned and skinned
1 [14–ounce] bottle Italian dressing
1/2 teaspoon hot sauce
1 teaspoon Worcestershire sauce
1/2 teaspoon lemon pepper
1/2 teaspoon garlic salt
1 tablespoon fresh chopped chives, or 1 1/2 teaspoons dried chives

• Arrange chicken breasts in a flat baking dish in a single layer.
• Mix remaining ingredients and pour over chicken; marinate for at least 1 hour in refrigerator.
• Bake 30 to 45 minutes at 350° until meat is tender, turning once during cooking.

Serve whole as an entrée or sliced as a part of a salad with leaf lettuce, sliced tomatoes, sliced cucumbers, and radishes with your choice of dressing.

❧ GREEK CHICKEN
Serves 6

6 chicken breast halves
1/4 cup lemon juice
1/4 cup olive oil
1/2 teaspoon salt
1/2 teaspoon pepper
1 teaspoon Worcestershire sauce
1 teaspoon oregano

• Arrange chicken, skin side up, in a single layer in a 9 x 13–inch baking dish.
• Mix lemon juice, oil, salt, pepper, Worcestershire sauce, and oregano. Pour mixture over the chicken and cover with foil.
• Bake for 30 minutes at 375°. Uncover.
• Bake an additional 25 to 30 minutes, or until chicken browns.

❧ CHICKEN À LA BRANDYWINE

Serves 6

6 chicken breast halves, boned and skinned
All-purpose flour
1/2 cup butter, melted and divided
Salt and pepper
3/4 cup sliced mushrooms
1/4 cup plus 1 tablespoon white wine
1 tablespoon brandy
1/4 cup chicken broth
2 teaspoons butter
1/4 cup shredded mozzerella cheese
1/4 cup grated Parmesan cheese

- Cut chicken breasts in half.
- Place each piece of chicken between two sheets of waxed paper; flatten to 1/8–inch thickness using a meat mallet.
- Dredge chicken lightly with flour. Place half of chicken in 3 tablespoons melted butter in a skillet; cook over low heat 3 to 4 minutes on each side or until golden brown.
- Place chicken in a greased 9–inch baking dish, overlapping edges; sprinkle with salt and pepper.
- Repeat procedure with remaining chicken, adding 3 tablespoons of butter to skillet. Reserve drippings in skillet.
- Sauté mushrooms in 2 tablespoons butter until tender; drain. Sprinkle evenly over chicken.
- Stir wine, brandy, and chicken broth into drippings in skillet.
- Simmer 7 minutes, stirring occasionally.
- Stir in a dash of salt, pepper, and 2 teaspoons butter. Spoon about half of sauce evenly over chicken, reserving remainder.
- Combine cheeses; sprinkle over chicken.
- Bake at 350° for 20 minutes.
- Place under broiler 1 to 2 minutes or until lightly browned.

Serve with warm reserved sauce.

This recipe, submitted by Chamsie Phillips, manager of the Museum Stores, has been a popular favorite of the museum staff and volunteers. It is a delicious and versatile dish that is always a hit at dinners, cocktail parties, and receptions.

∾ HERBAL STUFFED CHICKEN BREASTS

Serves 16; sliced, serves 24 as part of a buffet. Can be halved to serve 8

2 medium onions, finely chopped
2 tablespoons butter
2 [10–ounce] packages frozen chopped spinach, thawed and drained
2 [16–ounce] cartons whole-milk ricotta cheese
2 eggs, lightly beaten
1/2 cup coarsely chopped parsley
1 teaspoon each, dried or fresh summer savory, basil, tarragon, and oregano
Salt and freshly ground pepper to taste
Nutmeg to taste
16 boned chicken breast halves with skin on

- Sauté onions in butter until they are soft. Combine with other ingredients, except chicken, and mix well.
- Place each chicken breast skin up on a board, and trim away excess fat. Loosen skin from 1 side of the breast and stuff approximately 1/3 cup of filling under skin. Tuck skin under the breast, forming an even, round, dome shape. Season with salt and pepper to taste.
- Place stuffed breasts in two 9 x 13–inch buttered baking dishes. Bake for 30 to 35 minutes at 350°, or until golden brown. Do not overcook or chicken will be dry.
- Cool slightly before serving.
- If smaller serving pieces are desired, cool at room temperature before slicing; arrange on a platter and decorate with fresh herbs.

Delicious hot, warm, or cold, whole or sliced. May be frozen for later use.

104

❧ COQ AU VIN AVEC PINOT NOIR

Serves 4 to 6

1 chicken, cut in pieces
1 cup (or more) all-purpose flour
1/2 cup butter
2 tablespoons peanut oil
1 package pearl onions
8 slices bacon
1 to 2 [8–ounce] cans mushrooms, drained
1 tablespoon all-purpose flour (optional)
6 tablespoons brandy
3/4 bottle Pinot Noir
Salt and pepper to taste
Fresh chopped parsley

- Clean and dry chicken; dredge in flour. In a skillet, brown chicken in butter and peanut oil over medium-high heat. Remove from skillet and layer in the bottom of a 4–quart casserole or Dutch oven.
- Brown pearl onions in same pan. When golden, remove from pan and layer over chicken.
- Cut bacon strips into 1–inch pieces. Drain grease from skillet and brown bacon. When crispy, layer over onions.
- Layer mushrooms over bacon.
- Salt and pepper to taste.
- If you want a thicker sauce, sprinkle 1 tablespoon flour over ingredients in casserole.
- Heat brandy; pour over stew and flame. After flames subside, pour about 3/4 bottle Pinot Noir over, not allowing contents to be completely covered by liquid.
- Cover the casserole and bring to a boil; lower heat and simmer until cooked, about 45 minutes.

Serve over white rice, sprinkled with parsley.

Bernard Axel has been a premier chef in the Birmingham area for a number of years. His restaurant, Christian's, has had several locations, and recently moved to downtown Birmingham in the Tutwiler Hotel. From Christian's, we have a scrumptious recipe for Coq au Vin. This dish had its origins in provincial France, but this recipe places it on a level fit for kings. Classic ingredients and the tenderizing effect of the wine combine to make a flavorful and succulent dish you will want to serve often.

105

SESAME CHICKEN WITH GREEN NOODLES

Serves 4

4 chicken breast halves, boned and skinned
1/4 cup light brown sugar
1/3 cup soy sauce
1/4 cup dry sherry
2 tablespoons white wine vinegar
2 tablespoons sesame oil
1 teaspoon minced fresh ginger
1 clove garlic, minced
1/4 teaspoon black pepper
1/8 to 1/4 teaspoon red pepper
2 teaspoons cornstarch
1 sweet red pepper, cut into strips
1/4 cup sliced scallions
1 cup shredded red cabbage
1/2 cup coarsely chopped walnuts
2 tablespoons sesame seeds
2 tablespoons chopped fresh parsley
1 [8–ounce] package spinach noodles,
    prepared according to package directions

- Cut chicken into 3 x 1/2–inch strips; set aside.
- Combine brown sugar and the next 8 ingredients in a shallow 2–quart casserole. Add chicken and toss gently to coat. Cover and chill 30 minutes.
- Drain chicken, reserving 1/4 cup of the marinade. Return chicken to casserole.
- Combine reserved marinade and cornstarch. Pour over chicken.
- Cover and microwave on high for 3 to 6 minutes, or until chicken is done.
- Stir in remaining ingredients, except noodles. Let stand 1 minute.
- Serve over prepared noodles.

CHICKEN RIGGINS

Serves 8

4 whole chicken breasts
4 chicken thighs
Salt and pepper to taste
Celery leaves
3 tablespoons margarine
2 cups diced celery
1 cup diced onion
3 cups [12 ounces] shredded sharp Cheddar cheese
4 [1/2–ounce] packages sliced almonds
2 cups mayonnaise
2 teaspoons curry powder (optional)
Freshly prepared bread crumbs to taste

- In enough water to cover, cook chicken with salt, pepper, and celery leaves. Simmer until chicken is tender. Cool, bone, and dice.
- Sauté celery and onion in margarine.
- Combine chicken, celery, onion, cheese, mayonnaise, and almonds.
- Place in a 3–quart casserole. Top with bread crumbs and bake at 350° for 20 t0 25 minutes, or until casserole is golden brown.

Serve with green or fruit salad. May be served over rice.

In 1985, the museum opened the Critics' Room restaurant. It quickly became a popular downtown choice for lunch. Among the delicious sandwiches, soups, salads, and casseroles was the all-time favorite dish, Chicken Riggins. The recipe and name come from Wendell Riggins who opened and manages the restaurant. This rich and tasty casserole is easy to make and is an excellent dish to serve as part of a buffet or for a large dinner party.

❧ CHICKEN SPAGHETTI CASSEROLE

Serves 12

6 slices bacon, diced
10 large mushrooms, sliced
1 large onion, thinly sliced
1 [28–ounce] can crushed tomatoes
1 cup sliced pimento-stuffed green olives
1 teaspoon salt
1/2 teaspoon pepper
3 cups cooked, diced chicken
3 cups [12 ounces] grated medium Cheddar cheese
1 pound extra-thin spaghetti

- Brown bacon in a large skillet. Remove bacon and all but two tablespoons of drippings.
- Add mushrooms and onion slices to the skillet, and sauté until they are golden brown.
- Add bacon, tomatoes, olives, salt, and pepper. Bring to a boil and simmer for 10 minutes.
- Add chicken to the sauce.
- Cook spaghetti according to package directions, or until it is almost done; drain well.
- In a lightly-greased 9 x 13–inch baking dish, layer 1/2 of the spaghetti, the chicken sauce, and grated cheese; repeat layers. Bake for 1 hour at 350°. Cut into squares to serve.

❧ WHITE CHILI

Serves 12 to 16

2 pounds dried Great Northern white beans
3/4 tablespoon ground cumin
1 tablespoon ground oregano
1 tablespoon onion salt
1/2 tablespoon cayenne pepper
1/2 tablespoon seasoning salt
1/4 cup vegetable oil
1 1/2 cups diced onions
1 [27–ounce] can chopped mild green chile peppers
1 tablespoon minced garlic
4 quarts chicken stock
1 pint draft beer (12–ounce bottle will work)
4 pounds chicken breasts, boned and skinned

- Soak beans in cold water overnight.
- Mix cumin, oregano, salt, pepper, and seasoning salt together.
- Heat oil in a large stock pot and sauté onions until translucent. Add chilies, garlic, and half of seasoning mixture and sauté 1 minute longer.
- Drain beans and add beans, stock, and beer to pot.
- Bring to a boil, reduce heat, and simmer for about 2 hours, or until beans are tender.
- Wash chicken, place in a baking dish in a single layer, and sprinkle on other half of seasoning mixture. Bake at 350° for 15 minutes.
- Dice chicken into quarter-size pieces. Add to stock, simmer until chicken is done, another 5 to 10 minutes.

For a unusual variation of traditional chili, the Cabana Café has included their recipe for White Chili. This dish has the hot and spicy flavor of regular chili, but it is made with chicken, chicken broth, and white beans to give it the unique flavor and color. We recommend it highly for those cold winter days when you are looking for something different and delicious to make.

109

We close the section on poultry with two recipes for other-than-chicken poultry. They are from *The Modern Art of Cookery*, and, unlike Ragout of Chicken in a Bottle, will work just as well today as they did two hundred years ago. We have updated the instructions with contemporary terms and measurements, and recommend using a small turkey for the second recipe. Either dish makes a nice change from the usual chicken.

DUCK À LA MODE

Cut up a couple of ducks into quarters, and fry them in butter [*2 to 4 tablespoons*], of a light brown; pour out all the fat, and dust in a little flour [*about 1 tablespoon*]; then put in half a pint of strong gravy [*1 cup brown stock*], a gill of red wine [*1/2 cup*], two shalots, and an anchovy cut small [*optional*], with a faggot [*small bundle tied together*] of sweet herbs, and a little whole pepper; cover it close, and steam it for twenty minutes; take up your ducks into the dish you send them up in; strain your sauce, and scum [*skim*] it very clean; give it a boil up, with a bit of butter rolled in flour [*2 1–tablespoon balls coated heavily with flour*], till it is as thick as cream; pour it over your ducks, and send them to table garnished with orange or lemon.

[*We recommend making the gravy by mixing 2 tablespoons melted butter, or grease from the pan, with 2 tablespoons flour, stirring till smooth. Then slowly stir in the juices from the pan with water to equal 1 cup liquid, and the wine, shallots, and herbs; bring to a boil and cook, stirring, until thick. Add salt and pepper to taste.*]

A FOWL ROASTED WITH CHESTNUTS

Roast a quarter of a hundred of chestnuts [*place them on a baking tray with several tablespoons water, and bake at 350° for 10 to 15 minutes, until the shells can be peeled off*]; peel them; save out eight or ten, the rest bruise in a mortar [*process till coarsely chopped in a blender or food processor*], with the liver of the fowl [*optional, if you do not have it*], a quarter of a pound of ham well pounded [*processed with the chestnuts*], sweet herbs and parsley chopped fine [*to taste*]: Season it with mace, nutmeg, pepper and salt [*to taste*]: Mix all these together, and put them into the belly of your fowl: Spit it, and tie the neck and vent close [*truss it and place it on a roasting rack; bake at 325° until done, about 25 minutes per pound or until a meat thermometer placed in the center of the breast registers the finished temperature*]. Then for sauce, take the rest of the chestnuts, cut them in pieces, and put them into a good strong gravy [*1cup turkey or chicken stock plus clean pan juices from the cooked turkey*], with a glass of white wine [*1/2 cup*]: Thicken with a piece of butter rolled in flour [*see above recipe for recommended gravy instructions; season to taste with salt and pepper*]. When your fowl is done, dish it, and pour in the sauce. Garnish with orange and water cresses.

You may do a hen turkey in the same way.

MEATS

(Page 111) Robert Rauschenberg (American, born 1925), *Calf Startena*, 1977. Mixed media, 36 x 48 inches. Gift of Mr. and Mrs. Isadore Pizitz.

Calf Startena is one of six prints in the BMA permanent collection from the *Chow* series by Robert Rauschenberg. In these prints, Rauschenberg has irreverntly elevated common animal feed packages to the level of fine art.

Much of his work is done in mixed media, as in *Calf Startena* where he combined packaging for calf feed with pieces of fabric, stitching with heavy thread, and pencil drawings, and then a silk screen print over the assembled piece. Rauschenberg says he "tries to operate in the area between art and life." In this way he creates a tension between the real and the abstract by combining common, easily recognizable mass produced objects with abstract passages of color. His use of everyday objects calls attention to their legitimacy as works of art in themselves.

MEAT ENTRÉES

112

TO MAKE PIES THAT THE BIRDS MAY BE ALIVE IN THEM, AND FLIE OUT WHEN IT IS CUT UP

Make the coffin of a great pie or pastry, in the bottome thereof make a hole as big as your fist, or bigger if you will, let the sides of the coffin bee somewhat higher then ordinary pies, which done put it full of flower and bake it, and being baked, open the hole in the bottome, and take out the flower. Then having a pie of the bigness of the hole in the bottome of the coffin aforesaid, you shal put it into the coffin, withall put into the said coffin round about the aforesaid pie as many small live birds as the empty coffin will hold, besides the pie aforesaid. And this is to be done at such a time as you send the pie to the table, and set before the guests: where uncovering or cutting up the lid of the great pie, all the birds will flie out, which is to delight and pleasure shew to the company. And because they shall not bee altogether mocked, you shall cut open the small pie, and in this sort you may make many others, the like you may do with a tart.

TO DRESS LARKS PEAR FASHION

Truss your larks close, and cut off one leg; season them with mace, pepper and salt, and make a forcemeat thus: Take a veal sweet-bread, as much of beef suet, a few morels, and mushrooms; chop these very fine with a little lemon peel, and sweet herbs shred fine; mix all together, and moisten it with the yolk of an egg: Wrap up every lark in this force-meat, and shape it like a pear, leaving the leg for the stalk; wash them over with the yolk of an egg, and strew them over with bread crumbs; bake them in a gentle oven, of a fine brown; serve them up without sauce.

They are a good garnish for a fine made dish.

As with the last section, we start the meat recipes with two that are for your enjoyment rather than your guests. The first, from *The Delectable Past,* originated in Italy; but it was the English who made the dish so popular that a nursery rhyme was written about it. This version appeared in a 1598 English translation of a cookbook from 1518, Italy.

The second recipe comes from *The Modern Art of Cookery* and eighteenth-century England. Both attest to the creativity of cooks of the time, and most likely were used when a festive, large party was being held. We do not recommend trying these recipes at home. Anyone brave or flamboyant enough to make the attempt will have to calculate the ingredients and measurements on their own.

113

 STEAK BEIRUT

Serves 4

4 [1 1/2–inch thick] filet mignons
1 clove garlic
Juice of 1 lemon
1 [2–ounce] jar caviar
1 small onion, finely chopped

• Broil steaks on one side for 5 minutes.
• While steaks are broiling, rub a small bowl with cut clove of garlic.
• Add lemon juice, caviar, and onion to bowl. Mix well.
• Turn steaks and spread mixture on the uncooked side.
• Continue to broil for another 5 to 6 minutes.

MARVELOUS MARINATED ROAST

Serves 8

1 cup ketchup
2 teaspoons prepared mustard
1/2 teaspoon Worcestershire sauce
1 1/2 cups water
2 [0.7–ounce] envelopes Italian salad dressing mix
1 beef roast, 4 to 6 pounds

• Mix first 5 ingredients.
• Spear meat in several places, and put in a heavy duty zip-lock bag.
• Pour marinade over the meat and seal bag well.
• Place bag in a shallow pan and refrigerate for 8 hours, turning occasionally.
• Remove meat from bag, reserving marinade for basting and sauce.
• Place meat on a rack in a baking pan.
• Insert a meat thermometer.
• Bake at 425° for 30 to 40 minutes, or until the thermometer registers
  150° for medium-rare, or 160° for medium.
• Baste occasionally with marinade while baking.
• Boil reserved marinade for 2 minutes and serve with the roast.

◠ ROAST BEEF TENDERLOIN WITH MUSHROOM WINE SAUCE

Serves 8

1 [4–pound] beef tenderloin, trimmed
2 cups dry white wine
2 tablespoons melted butter
3 tablespoons caraway seeds
Salt
Black pepper, freshly ground
1 pound mushrooms, thinly sliced
1/2 cup butter, melted
2 tablespoons chopped fresh parsley
Salt
Black pepper, freshly ground
1 to 2 tablespoons cornstarch or all-purpose flour (optional)

- Marinate tenderloin in wine for 8 hours in refrigerator (in a non-metallic container). Turn often.
- Preheat oven to 425°.
- Remove roast from wine, reserving wine, and pat it dry.
- Place roast in a roasting pan and brush with melted butter.
- Press caraway seeds onto the roast, and season with salt and pepper.
- Insert a meat thermometer and cook until it registers 140° for rare, 150° for medium rare, 160° for medium, 170° for well done.
- Place cooked roast on serving platter and let rest 15 minutes before carving.
- Meanwhile, prepare sauce by melting butter in a large skillet; add mushrooms and cook for 5 minutes, stirring often.
- In a heavy saucepan, bring reserved wine to a boil and reduce to about 1 1/2 cups.
- Pour reduced wine into roasting pan, stirring to deglaze pan.
- Return wine to the saucepan and cook for 2 to 3 minutes over high heat. Add cornstarch, if sauce is too thin, stirring until it begins to bubble.
- Add mushroom mixture.
- Carve roast into very thin slices and spoon some of sauce on each serving.

Roquefort Potatoes au Gratin make an excellent accompaniment for this dish.

This recipe comes from Susan Rouse, who claims it is well worth the extra time and effort required. She says it is always a hit when she prepares it for special company. The carraway-seed flavor offers a pleasant surprise.

115

❧ ROBUST SAUSAGE–BEEF CASSEROLE

Serves 8 to 10

1 pound sweet Italian sausage, cut into pieces
1 pound boneless beef chuck, cut into 1–inch pieces
2 large onions, sliced
2 medium cloves garlic, minced
2 medium green peppers, each cut into 8 strips
4 to 6 medium potatoes, quartered
2 [15–ounce] cans dried red kidney beans, drained, reserving 1 cup liquid
1 teaspoon dried basil
1/2 teaspoon salt
1/4 teaspoon pepper
1 cup beef stock

- Brown sausage and beef; place meat in a 6–quart casserole.
- Add remaining ingredients. Pour in stock and kidney bean liquid.
- Cover, and bake at 350° for 1 hour and 15 minutes, stirring occasionally.

Great to freeze and keep on hand for last minute company.

❧ CABERNET BEEF STEW

Serves 4 to 6

1 1/2 to 2 pounds boneless beef stew meat
1 stalk celery, or 1/2 cup chopped celery
1 onion, sliced
4 carrots, cut into large pieces
1 [16–ounce] can crushed tomatoes
3 to 4 small potatoes, peeled and cut in half
1/4 cup Cabernet or other red wine
3 tablespoons tapioca
3 tablespoons Worcestershire sauce
1/2 teaspoon basil
1/2 teaspoon oregano
1/4 teaspoon marjoram
1 bay leaf
Salt and pepper to taste

- Place beef into a 4–quart oven-proof casserole.
- Add remaining ingredients, including spices.
- Cover and bake at 250° for 6 hours.

TO DRESS VEAL À LA BOURGEOISE

Cut your veal in pretty thick slices off the fillet [*1 pound veal tenderloin, cut in slices or 1–inch cubes*]; lard them with bacon [*optional*], and season them with pepper, salt, mace, nutmeg, and shred parsley [*to taste*]; cut some slices of bacon [*3 or 4*], and lay them in the bottom of a stew-pan, and the veal upon them. Cover it, and set it over a slow fire [*medium heat*] for six or eight minutes; then brisk up the fire [*turn heat to high*], and brown your veal on both sides; shake some flour over it [*1 1/2 to 2 tablespoons*], and as soon as it begins to brown, pour in a quart of good veal broth warm [*chicken or beef stock will work also*]. Cover it close, and stew it gently [*reduce heat*], till you think it is enough [*1 hour*]; then take out the slices of bacon, and scum off [*skim*] all the fat very clean: Beat up the yolks of three eggs in a little gravy; mix all together, and keep it stirring one way till it is smooth, and of a proper thickness. Squeeze in a little lemon [*juice of 1/2 to 1 lemon*]; dish up your veal, and pour your sauce over. Garnish the dish with orange or lemon.

Another recipe from *The Modern Art of Cookery* is delicious with a little updating. It is for what we would probably term a veal stew. It is possible to leave the veal in slices, but we found it also turned out well when cut in 1-inch cubes. This dish is also delicious with the addition of a half pound of your favorite fresh mushrooms the last 20 minutes of cooking.

MARINATED VEAL CHOPS

Serves 2

2 [12–ounce] veal chops, trimmed close
Salt and pepper to taste
1/2 cup smooth peanut butter
2 tablespoons melted margarine

- Purchase center cut loin veal chops, approximately 12 ounces each.
- Salt and pepper veal chops and spread peanut butter evenly over chops.
- With a wet fork, puncture the chops all over. Let chops stand overnight in refrigerator.
- Grill over a hot oak fire about 5 to 6 minutes per side. Baste with melted margarine.
- Serve with baked acorn squash and seasoned wild rice.

This recipe also works well with pork chops.

One of the more unusual meat dishes in this cookbook comes from Zelda's restaurant on Seventh Avenue South in the Lakeview district of Southside. The marinade and subsequent flavor are what make this dish unusual, but this is also a wonderfully easy dish to prepare.

117

❧ LEMON VEAL WITH ARTICHOKE HEARTS

Serves 4

1 pound veal scallopini slices, 1/4–inch thick
1/4 cup all-purpose flour, divided
1/4 teaspoon salt
2 to 3 tablespoons butter or margarine
1/4 cup water
Juice of 2 lemons
2 tablespoons Worcestershire sauce
1 cup chicken broth
1/4 cup dry vermouth
1 teaspoon dried whole marjoram
1/2 teaspoon minced garlic
1 bay leaf
1 [14–ounce] can artichoke hearts, drained
Hot cooked fettucini
Lemon slices and parsley for garnish

- Combine 3 tablespoons of flour with salt and pepper; dredge veal in the mixture.
- Melt butter in a large skillet over medium heat. Add veal, cook for 1 minute on each side to brown; remove and drain on paper towels.
- Stir 1 tablespoon of flour into 1/4 cup of water. Add flour mixture, lemon juice, Worcestershire sauce, broth, vermouth, marjoram, garlic, and bay leaf to skillet; bring to a boil, stirring often.
- Add veal and artichokes; cover, reduce heat, and simmer for about 5 minutes. Discard bay leaf.
- Serve over pasta; garnish with lemon slices and parsley.

❧ VEAL SCALLOPINI À LA MARSALA

Serves 6

1 to 1 1/2 pounds veal scallopini
1/2 cup all-purpose flour
4 tablespoons unsalted butter
4 tablespoons olive oil
Juice of 1 lemon
3/4 cup Marsala wine
Salt and freshly ground pepper to taste
Fresh sprigs of thyme for garnish

- Lightly coat each veal scallopini with flour.
- In a large skillet, heat butter with the oil until it is very hot but not smoking. Quickly brown veal on both sides.
- Lower heat to medium and add lemon juice and Marsala wine. Simmer for 4 to 5 minutes. Sprinkle with salt and pepper.
- Serve immediately, garnished with thyme.

 ## OSSO BUCO

Serves 6

3 whole veal shanks, cut into 3–inch pieces each
All-purpose flour for dredging
1/4 cup olive oil
1 onion, thinly sliced
1 bay leaf
2 small carrots, thinly sliced
1 stalk celery, diced
1/2 cup dry white wine
2 1/2 cups canned tomatoes, undrained
1 1/2 tablespoons chopped fresh parsley
1 clove garlic, crushed
1 tablespoon grated lemon peel
Salt and freshly ground pepper to taste

- Dredge shanks with flour.
- Heat oil in a heavy skillet; add shanks and brown on all sides. Remove to a warm platter.
- Add more oil to the skillet if necessary. Add onion, bay leaf, carrots, and celery. Cook over medium heat for 5 minutes.
- Add wine, and simmer until all wine is evaporated.
- Return shanks to skillet and add tomatoes. Cover and simmer until tender, about 1 1/2 hours. Add a small amount of wine if necessary.
- Remove shanks from the skillet and strain sauce. Remove bones from shanks, and return shanks and sauce to skillet. Stir in parsley, garlic, lemon peel, salt and pepper. Simmer 5 minutes longer.
- Serve over rice with parsley garnish.

Mrs. Ruth S. Engle and her family discovered this recipe while traveling in Italy. The kids loved it and they have all been testing and refining it ever since. This is the version they all like best.

119

Our next two recipes are, again, from *The Modern Art of Cookery* in the museum's Chellis Library collection. And again we have updated the measurements and instructions in brackets. The pork cutlets are delicious broiled or grilled, and the sauce may be made from scratch or by using a ready-made gravy and enhancing the taste according to the recipe. The Devonshire Squab Pye is delicious with just a top crust and a thicker sauce, so we have adjusted the recipe instructions to reflect these changes. A simple way to thicken stock is to put 1 tablespoon of flour in a jar or container with a cover, add 2 to 3 tablespoons water, cover, and shake till liquid is smooth with no lumps; then slowly pour into hot stock, stirring until it is thickened. We have also substituted the original mutton, whence came the name, with pork, more to twentieth-century American tastes. We hope you find these two dishes as delicious as we do.

120

 ## TO DRESS PORK CUTLETS

Take the skin off a loin of pork, and cut it into cutlets [*purchase 1 to 1 1/2 pounds pork cutlets at the butchers*]; season them with sage, parsly, and thyme cut small, pepper, salt, [*all to taste*] and crumbs of bread [*about 1/2 cup total*]; broil them a fine brown; take half a pint of good gravy [*1 cup, or 1 cup stock thickened with 1 tablespoon flour disolved in 1/4 cup water*], a spoonful of made mustard [*1 tablespoon Dijon-style mustard*], and a piece of butter rolled in flour, to thicken it [*you may use this method to thicken, or see suggestion at left*]. Shred two shalots very fine [*add shallots to taste*], and put it to your sauce, with a little vinegar [*1 tablespoon*]. Dish up your cutlets, pour the sauce over them, and serve them hot to table.

 ## A DEVONSHIRE SQUAB PYE

Make a good crust, and sheet your dish all over [*we suggest using a top crust only; puff pastry p. 78*]; lay a layer of pippins [*cooking apples; you will need 2 apples, peeled, cored, and sliced thin*], and strew sugar over them [*1 tablespoon brown sugar*]; cut a loin of mutton into steaks, season them with pepper and salt [*1 to 1 1/4 pound boneless pork cutlets; brown them in a skillet with 1 to 2 tablespoons butter*]; lay a layer of steaks, then pipins; then lay some onions sliced thin on the apples [*sauté the onions till translucent in the skillet used to cook the meat*]; then the rest of your mutton [*pork*], and apples and onions over all; pour in a pint of water [*1 cup gravy, or stock thickened with 1 tablespoon flour, plus 1/2 cup white wine*], and lid your pye; let it be well baked. [*Bake at 350° for 35 to 45 minutes, until crust is golden.*]

HERBED PORK TENDERLOIN WITH LEMON CAPER SAUCE

Serves 4 to 6

1 [1 1/2– to 2–pound] whole boneless pork tenderloin
3 ounces roasted red peppers, whole pimentos, or sun-dried tomatoes*
1 clove garlic
Salt and pepper to taste
4 sprigs fresh rosemary
3 slices bacon, cut in half
1/4 to 1/2 cup herb seasoned bread crumbs
Butcher's twine
Lemon Caper Sauce (recipe follows)

- Slice the loin lengthwise, three-fourths of the way through.
- Rub inside and out with the cut garlic clove. Lightly sprinkle the inside with salt and pepper. Lay rosemary sprigs in the cavity. Fill it with peppers, pimentos, or tomatoes.
- Pull the loin together and lay six pieces of bacon across the opening. Secure with twine.
- Sprinkle the herb seasoned bread crumbs over the top.
- Insert a meat thermometer, and bake at 350° or until the thermometer reaches 170°.
- Remove from oven and let stand for 5 to 10 minutes.
- Carefully remove twine, and slice.

To enhance flavor, soak dried tomatoes in warm water.

Lemon Caper Sauce

2 tablespoons butter
2 tablespoons flour
1 cup chicken stock
2 eggs, beaten
Juice of one lemon
2 tablespoons water
Salt and pepper to taste
1 tablespoon capers, drained

- Melt butter in a medium sauce pan, add flour and cook over meduim-low heat for 2 minutes.
- Remove from heat, gradually stir in chicken stock, then eggs.
- Return to heat. Cook over medium heat, stirring constantly until thickened.
- Remove from heat, stir in lemon juice and capers. If too thick, use water a little at a time to thin to desired consistency. Season with salt and pepper.

For those who prefer a no-fat version, we include the following recipe:

A no-fat basic white sauce

1 cup water
2 tablespoons flour
5 tablespoons non-fat dry milk powder
1 teaspoon butter sprinkles
1/2 cup egg substitute

- Combine water, flour, milk powder, and butter sprinkles. Shake to blend.
- Add egg substitute and cook.
- Then add capers and lemon.

121

❧ PORK IN SOUR CREAM WITH CAPERS

Serves 3 to 4

1 pork tenderloin, cut in 1–inch slices, or 4 pork chops
2 tablespoons butter
1 tablespoon oil
Salt and freshly ground pepper
1/2 cup beef broth
2 tablespoons Dijon mustard
3 tablespoons all-purpose flour
1 tablespoon water
1 cup sour cream
3 tablespoons capers

- Brown pork in the oil and butter; season with salt and pepper.
- Combine mustard and stock and pour it over the meat.
- Cover, reduce heat, and simmer, for 1 hour.
- Remove the pork.
- Mix the flour with the water to make a paste, and stir it into the liquid in the pot. Cook, stirring, until the sauce thickens.
- Add sour cream and capers, heating until warm. Pour sauce over pork.

Good served over rice or noodles, garnished with roasted red pepper slices or pimento strips.

❧ PROVOCATIVE PORK TENDERLOINS

Serves 4 to 6

2 pork tenderloins [1 3/4 to 2 pounds total weight]
1 cup pineapple preserves
1/4 cup Dijon mustard
1 tablespoon prepared horseradish
1 tablespoon soy sauce

- Mix all the ingredients together, except the pork tenderloins, and divide in half.
- Brush 1/2 of the mixture on top of each tenderloin.
- Place tenderloins in a small broiling pan [8 x 12 inches]. Bake at 375° for 15 to 20 minutes or until meat thermometer reaches 165° to 170°. Baste after 10 minutes.
- Remove roast from oven; let it stand for 5 to 10 minutes before slicing.
- Heat remaining sauce and serve with the meat.

You can double sauce ingredients if you wish extra sauce; leftover sauce keeps well in the refrigerator.

∽ SWEET AND SOUR PORK

Serves 2 to 4 as main course, 4 to 6 as a side dish

1 egg, beaten
1/4 cup tapioca or cornstarch
1/4 cup all-purpose flour
2 tablespoons soy sauce
1 pound lean boneless pork, cut into thin strips
3 cups vegetable oil for frying
2 tablespoons vegetable oil
2 teaspoons minced garlic
1 large green pepper, cut into 1/2 inch squares
1 medium carrot, julienned
6 tablespoons vinegar
6 tablespoons sugar
6 tablespoons water
6 tablespoons ketchup
1/2 teaspoon salt
1 1/2 teaspoons tapioca or cornstarch

- Combine egg, cornstarch, flour, and soy sauce and coat pork.
- Heat 3 cups of oil to 375°. Deep fry pork. Remove to an ovenproof dish and keep warm in oven.
- Pour out remaining oil.
- Add 2 tablespoons of oil to the pan, and heat for 30 seconds. Add garlic, stir, then add green pepper and carrot. Stir fry for 3 minutes.
- Combine vinegar, sugar, water, ketchup, salt, and starch. Pour over vegetables, and mix well. Add pork and toss.
- Serve immediately.

Serve with hot rice.

Our next recipe from Buttiker's Café is another quick contemporary dish, but one that is filled with flavor. For a minimum of time and effort, your results are gourmet quality. Again we stress the use of the freshest ingredients for maximum flavor.

124

Zelda's second recipe is also for quick and contemporary lamb chops. Again the use of unusual ingredients offers a surprise in a dish that will delight the taste buds. With a flavor that contrasts with Lamb Chops Montrachet, Zelda's Lamb Chops are deliciously unusual, but like the other, are grilled for cooking ease. We hope you will enjoy these two alternative lamb chop recipes often.

☙ LAMB CHOPS MONTRACHET

Serves 4

8 double bone lamb chops, Frenched, or 16 single bone chops
3 tablespoons olive oil
3 to 4 cloves garlic, finely chopped
12 ounces fresh mushrooms, sliced
1 tablespoon Dijon mustard
1 1/2 cups Burgundy wine
8 artichokes, canned
Salt and pepper to taste
Sprig of fresh rosemary

- Grill lamb chops medium rare and heat artichokes.
- Meanwhile heat olive oil; add garlic, mushrooms, and mustard.
- Cook, stirring over low heat for 1 minute; add Burgundy, artichoke juice, and rosemary.
- Simmer until sauce is reduced to half and season with salt and pepper.
- Arrange lamb chops and artichokes on a serving platter, pour sauce over, and garnish with fresh rosemary sprigs.

☙ ZELDA'S LAMB CHOPS

Serves 2

4 lamb chops [4 to 6 ounces each]
6 ounces feta cheese
1/2 cup butter cut into butter pats
Salt and pepper to taste

- Cut excess fat from lamb chops and season with salt and pepper. Using a paring knife, form a pocket in the large end of chop.
- Let feta cheese come to room temperature. Pack pocket with feta cheese.
- Place stuffed chop on open fire of oak, very hot, approximately 3 to 4 minutes per side.
- Add salt and pepper and a pat of butter.

Serve with fresh steamed vegetables and boiled new potatoes.

❧ LAMB SHANKS À L'ORANGE

Serves 2

3/4 cup orange juice
2 tablespoons teriyaki sauce
1 tablespoon Worcestershire sauce
1 teaspoon garlic powder
2 large lamb shanks

- Combine orange juice, sauces, and garlic powder; pour over lamb shanks.
- Bake in a covered roasting pan at 325° for 1 1/2 hours, or until done.
- Serve with orange slices and sprigs of parsley.

125

∽ MEAT LOAF TERIYAKI

Serves 6 to 8

2 pounds lean ground beef
2 eggs, lightly beaten
1/2 cup bread crumbs
1/2 cup finely chopped green pepper
1 medium onion, finely chopped
1 clove garlic, crushed
2 tablespoons soy sauce
2 tablespoons brown sugar
2 tablespoons fresh lemon juice
1 tablespoon fresh parsley
3/4 teaspoon ground ginger
1/2 cup brown sugar
1/2 cup soy sauce

- Combine all the ingredients except brown sugar and soy sauce. Form into a loaf and place in a loaf pan coated lightly with cooking spray.
- Bake at 350° for 1 hour. Baste often with a mixture of 1/2 cup brown sugar and 1/2 cup soy sauce.
- Heat remaining basting sauce, and serve it with the sliced meat loaf.

∽ ESTELLE'S STUFFED PEPPERS

Serves 6

6 bell peppers
1 pound ground beef
1 medium onion, finely chopped
1/2 teaspoon salt
1/2 teaspoon pepper
1/2 cup cooked rice
2 [16–ounce] cans sauerkraut, drained and well-rinsed
2 [16–ounce] cans tomatoes
1 [10 1/2–ounce] can condensed tomato soup
1/3 cup brown sugar
1/3 cup sugar

126

This recipe started as a mistake. Bette Blumenthal's mother had been given a delicious recipe for stuffed cabbage, but accidentally used green peppers instead. The results were so delicious, they have been enjoying the dish ever since.

- Wash peppers and remove the tops, seeds, and pulp (if using large peppers, cut them in half).
- Mix beef, onion, salt, pepper, and rice.
- Stuff peppers with meat mixture.
- Place peppers upright in a large pot. If using halves, place pepper side down.
- Cover peppers with sauerkraut.
- Pour tomatoes, tomato soup, and brown and white sugar over peppers and sauerkraut.
- Cover pot and simmer for 1 hour 15 minutes.

☙ SUNDAY NIGHT STEW

Serves 4 to 6

1 1/2 pounds ground sirloin
6 medium carrots, peeled and thickly sliced
6 stalks celery, thickly sliced
6 or 8 fresh tomatoes, peeled and chopped, or 2 [15–ounce] cans tomatoes
1 cup chicken broth
2 tablespoons dried parsley flakes
1 tablespoon paprika
1 tablespoon dried thyme
1 tablespoon dried marjoram
1/4 cup dried chopped onion
Garlic powder to taste
Salt and pepper to taste

- Form ground sirloin into golf-ball-size meat balls.
- Place carrots and celery in the bottom of a Dutch oven and top with tomatoes.
- Cover vegetables with chicken broth.
- Place meat balls in a single layer over vegetables.
- Sprinkle remaining 7 ingredients over the meat balls.
- Bring to a boil. Cover, reduce to low heat, and cook for 1 hour 15 minutes.
- Add water as needed.

Good make ahead dish

Blue & White Café in Mountain Brook Village has long been known for their catering and delicious soups, sandwiches, salads, and desserts. They have given us a delightful recipe that is a traditional favorite, but uses "Ultra Lean" beef for health-conscious consumers. The use of this meat combines with a superb recipe for chili that will please all tastes.

◦➔ BLUE & WHITE'S "ULTRA LEAN" CHILI

Serves 12 to 16

2 pounds "ultra-lean" ground beef*
2 large green peppers, diced
2 large white or yellow onions, diced
2 [16–ounce] cans tomato sauce
4 [16–ounce] cans tomatoes
6 [16–ounce] cans red kidney beans, undrained
2 tablespoons lemon juice
1/4 cup brown sugar
3 tablespoons chili powder
1 tablespoon crushed red pepper flakes
Grated Cheddar cheese and chopped green onion for garnish

- Brown ground beef, onions, and pepper in a large Dutch oven until nicely browned, adding a tablespoon or two of water, if neccessary, but no oil.
- Reduce heat and add tomato sauce, tomatoes, and kidney beans.
- Cook over low heat, stirring often, and adding water when needed, for 1 hour.
- Add lemon juice, brown sugar, and chili pepper and crushed red pepper to taste.
- Simmer for 30 minutes more, stirring often and adding more water as needed.
- Serve garnished with grated Cheddar cheese and chopped onion.

Goes well with green salad and cornbread.
Recipe can be halved

"Ultra-Lean" is the brand name of ground beef developoed at Auburn for McDonald's McLean burger. Sold in the Birmingham area exclusively by Bruno's.

∾ SOUTHERN HAM SANDWICHES

Amounts used depends on number serving and quantities desired

Ham, hand-sliced thinly
Fresh collard greens, steamed or boiled
Whole wheat or multi-grain bread, sliced
Butter or margarine
Mayonnaise
Mustard, grained
Pepper sauce or hot sauce (optional)

- Fry ham slices in oil or butter until crisp on the edges.
- Steam or boil fresh collard greens until just barely tender. Drain well and pat dry.
- Toast bread on both sides and spread it lightly with butter, mayonnaise, and mustard.
- Fill sandwich with ham and warm greens. Add a little pepper sauce or hot sauce, if desired. The sandwich should be warm, somewhat moist, and thick.
- Cut the sandwich in half and serve it with your favorite ice-cold beer.

While getting ready to test submitted recipes, everyone on the volunteer committee agreed that Donald Comer was "putting us on" when we read this one. But we decided to be fair and test it anyway. Were we surprised! It is one of the best submitted; a true taste of the South, and healthy, too.

❧ MUFFULETTA SANDWICHES

Serves 6

1 1/2 cups chopped pimento-stuffed green olives
1 [4 1/2–ounce] can chopped black olives
1/3 cup olive oil
1/3 cup chopped parsley
3 anchovy fillets, mashed
2 tablespoons capers
1 tablespoon minced garlic
1 tablespoon oregano
Pepper to taste
1 loaf Italian bread
1/2 pound salami or ham, thinly sliced
1/2 pound provolone, mortadilla, or mozzarella cheese, thinly sliced

- Mix first 9 ingredients in a bowl; cover and let stand.
- Split Italian bread horizontally and hollow it out. Mound half of the olive mixture on bottom half of bread; layer meat and cheese alternately. Mound the other half of the olive mixture in the top portion of the bread.
- Carefully press the two sections of bread firmly together. Wrap in plastic wrap and press again. Cut in 2– or 3–inch wedges to serve.

A fabulous picnic sandwich

PASTA, RICE, & GRAINS

(Page 131) Panel, China, Qing dynasty (1644–1912). Lacquer and wood, 26 1/4 x 20 3/4 inches. Gift of Mr. and Mrs. William M. Spencer III.

Carved lacquer panels of the Qing dynasty are masterpieces of artistry and skill. Numerous layers of lacquer were applied to such panels before the craftsman could carve the rich, intricate designs. The depiction of air, water, and earth were accomplished in panels such as this with standard, stylized patterns, while a sense of spacial perspective was obtained through the deep undercutting of the various figures and design elements.

132

❧ BLACK BEAN LASAGNA

Serves 8

2 [16–ounce] cans black beans
5 tablespoons olive oil
1 medium onion, chopped
4 cloves garlic, minced
3 cups tomato puree
2 cups crushed tomatoes
1 teaspoon sugar
1 teaspoon oregano
1 1/2 teaspoons salt
1/2 teaspoon pepper
1 bay leaf
2 cups cottage cheese
1 egg, beaten
1/2 cup fresh coriander or cilantro
1 cup grated Parmesan cheese
9 lasagna noodles, cooked according to package directions
4 cups [16 ounces] shredded mozzarella cheese

- Purée beans in a blender with 2 tablespoons of olive oil.
- Sauté onions and garlic in 3 tablespoons olive oil.
- Add tomato purée, crushed tomatoes, sugar, oregano, salt, pepper, and bay leaf and simmer for 30 minutes. Remove bay leaf.
- In a bowl, combine cottage cheese, egg, coriander or cilantro, and 1/2 cup grated Parmesan cheese.
- Lightly grease a 9 x 13–inch baking dish with cooking spray.
- Arrange 3 noodles on the bottom of dish. Spread 1/3 of the cottage cheese mixture, 1/3 of the tomato and bean mixture, cover with 1/3 of the mozzarella, and sprinkle with 1/3 of the remaining Parmesan cheese.
- Repeat these layers twice.
- Bake at 375° for 30 minutes, until bubbling.

133

PASTA WITH WALNUT AND BASIL SAUCE

Serves 4

2 cups fresh basil, packed
2 large cloves garlic
1 small tomato, peeled and seeded
1/4 cup grated Parmesan cheese
5 tablespoons olive oil
Salt and pepper to taste
12 ounces fresh or 8 ounces dry pasta, cooked al denté
3 tablespoons heavy cream
1/2 cup coarsely chopped walnuts
Fresh basil leaves and Parmesan to garnish

- In a blender or food processor, combine basil, garlic, tomato, and Parmesan cheese.
- Process to a smooth paste.
- Add olive oil, a drop at a time, until all oil is incorporated.
- Season to taste.
- Toss hot pasta with the cream, basil sauce, and walnuts.
- Garnish with fresh basil leaves and Parmesan.
- Serve immediately.

FETTUCINE ALFREDO

Serves 6

1 1/2 cups heavy cream
1 1/2 cups grated fresh Parmesan cheese
1/2 cup butter
2 egg yolks, lightly beaten
Salt to taste
White pepper to taste
1 pound spinach fettucine noodles

- Heat cream in a heavy pan.
- As cream begins to simmer, gradually stir in cheese; continue cooking and stirring for 10 minutes.
- Add butter slowly, stirring as you add.
- When sauce is smooth, remove it from the heat.
- Beat a small amount of sauce into the egg yolks to warm them, then add the yolk mixture to the sauce, stirring with a whisk.
- Season with salt and pepper.
- Boil the noodles in salted water with a little olive oil added, about 10 minutes or until they are al denté.
- Drain noodles quickly, pour sauce over, and serve immediately.

❧ PASTA WITH GORGONZOLA SAUCE

Serves 6

1 tablespoon butter or margarine
2 cups [8 ounces] sliced mushrooms
3/4 cup half-and-half
5 ounces Gorgonzola cheese, crumbled
3/4 cup chicken broth
10 ounces spinach fettucine
1/2 pound tiny shrimp, cooked and shelled
2 tablespoons minced parsley
Freshly-ground pepper to taste

- Melt butter in an 8 or 10-inch pan and sauté the mushrooms.
- Add half-and-half, cheese, and broth.
- Stir until cheese melts, being careful not to boil; keep warm.
- In a pot with 3 quarts of salted, boiling water, cook pasta, uncovered, for 7 minutes. Drain.
- Combine pasta, sauce, and shrimp.
- Gently toss with 2 forks until pasta absorbs most of the liquid (about 4 minutes).
- Serve topped with parsley and ground pepper.

For a variation: Use larger shrimp and serve as an entree with a green salad and rolls.

135

∾ LINGUINE WITH WHITE CLAM SAUCE

Serves 4

1/3 cup oil (part light oil and part virgin olive oil; all olive oil is too heavy)
1 large onion, chopped
3 small cloves garlic, minced
3 tablespoons all-purpose flour
1/2 teaspoon grated nutmeg
1/2 teaspoon basil
1/2 teaspoon dried, crushed oregano
1/4 teaspoon salt
1/8 teaspoon white pepper
1 bay leaf
1 teaspoon grated fresh lemon peel
1 cup chopped fresh parsley, divided
2 [6 1/2–ounce] cans minced clams
2 tablespoons fresh lemon juice
1 cup water
8 ounces linguine
Parmesan cheese

- Heat oil in a heavy pan over medium heat; sauté onions until soft. Stir in garlic and sauté 2 minutes longer.
- Stir in flour, seasonings, and 1/2 cup parsley; cook, stirring, for 2 or 3 minutes.
- Drain clams, reserving the juice.
- Heat clam juice and water, being careful not to boil.
- Add onion and stir; then add clams and lemon juice.
- Simmer very gently for 5 minutes.
- Stir in the remaining parsley.
- Serve over cooked linguine, garnished with grated Parmesan.

∾ TOMATO LINGUINE WITH SHRIMP

Serves 4

12 ounces tomato linguine
1/2 pound snow peas or fresh green beans
2 tablespoons butter
1 red pepper, cut into thin strips
1 pound large shrimp, peeled and deveined
1 clove garlic, crushed
2 tablespoons fresh dill, chopped
Freshly ground pepper to taste
1 lemon, cut in half
3/4 cup dry white wine
Fresh dill sprigs

- Cook linguine according to package directions. Drain and keep warm.
- Steam or cook snow peas or beans in a small amount of water until just tender, about 5 minutes.
- Meanwhile, melt butter in a large skillet and stir in crushed garlic.
- Add red pepper and sauté until tender, about 2 to 3 minutes. Remove from pan.
- Add shrimp, sprinkle with dill and pepper, and sauté until they begin to turn golden pink, turning to cook evenly, about 3 to 4 minutes.
- Squeeze on juice of 1/2 lemon and add wine. Cook until shrimp are done, another 4 to 5 minutes.
- Meanwhile, arrange red pepper strips and snow peas or beans in a fan shape on 4 plates. Divide linguine into 4 portions and mound next to vegetables.
- Slice 4 thin slices from remaining half of lemon, and make one cut in each from edge to center of slice.
- Remove shrimp from pan and continue to cook sauce until it is reduced by 1/3.
- Arrange shrimp around linguine.
- Pour sauce over shrimp and linguine and garnish with twisted lemon slices and dill sprigs; serve.

137

∾ PASTA CARBONARA

Serves 4

1/2 pound sliced bacon
2 cloves garlic, chopped
2 eggs, beaten
1 cup evaporated skim milk
1/4 cup grated Parmesan cheese
6 or 7 ounces of linguine
Chopped parsley and Parmesan cheese for garnish

- Cook bacon and garlic in skillet; drain on paper towels.
- Drain skillet, and wipe it with a paper towel.
- In the same pan, combine eggs with milk and cook, stirring, over medium heat, until the mixture coats a metal spoon.
- Stir in bacon mixture and Parmesan cheese. Heat through.
- Pour over hot, cooked pasta, and toss to coat.
- Sprinkle with parsley and more Parmesan. Serve on a warm platter.

∾ THREE PEPPER PASTA

Serves 4

3 tablespoons olive oil
10 spring onions, including green tops
1 purple onion, chopped
1 red pepper, chopped
1 green pepper, chopped
1 yellow pepper, chopped
1 clove garlic, minced
4 ounces Stilton cheese, crumbled
9 ounces angel hair pasta

- Heat olive oil in a heavy skillet.
- Add onions and peppers.
- Sauté over medium heat for 4 minutes.
- Add garlic and sauté an additional 3 to 4 minutes.
- Remove from heat.
- Stir in crumbled cheese.
- Serve over cooked and well-drained pasta.

PASTA WITH ONIONS AND MUSHROOMS

Serves 6

2 medium-sized sweet onions
5 tablespoons butter, divided
1 pound fresh mushrooms, sliced
1 teaspoon salt
1/4 teaspoon freshly ground pepper
1/4 teaspoon freshly grated nutmeg
3 tablespoons chopped fresh parsley
2 teaspoons chopped fresh basil
1/2 cup dry white wine
1 cup cream
1 pound thin spaghetti or angel hair pasta
4 slices bacon
Freshly grated Parmesan cheese

- Peel and slice onions very thin.
- Melt 3 tablespoons of butter in a large skillet and sauté onions until translucent. Cover the skillet and cook the onions for 1 hour over very low heat, stirring occasionally. They should be a golden brown color when done.
- Wash, dry, and slice mushrooms. Sauté them in the remaining 2 tablespoons butter until tender.
- Season with salt, pepper, and nutmeg, and add 2 tablespoons of parsley and basil.
- Add mixture to the onions and pour in wine. Cook for 5 to 10 minutes.
- Cook pasta according to package directions.
- Fry bacon until crisp and drain on a paper towel.
- Five minutes before serving, add cream to the onion/mushroom mixture and heat through, being careful not to boil.
- Place pasta in a warm serving dish and pour the onion/mushroom mixture over. Toss lightly.
- Garnish with crumbled bacon pieces and remaining tablespoon of parsley.

Serve hot with grated Parmesan cheese.

139

∾ SUMMER RIGATONI

Serves 4

1/2 tablespoon oil
12 asparagus spears, cut in 1–inch lengths
3 carrots, cut in thin strips
1/2 small onion, chopped
3/4 cup chicken bouillon
1/2 pound smoked turkey breast, cut into strips
2 cups heavy cream
1 teaspoon sage
1 teaspoon garlic powder
1/2 teaspoon black pepper
Approximately 2 tablespoons fresh Parmesan cheese to thicken sauce
8 ounces rigatoni
1/4 cup chopped pecans
Fresh Parmesan cheese for garnish

- Sauté asparagus, carrots, and onion in oil until they are barely tender.
- Stir in bouillon and bring to a boil.
- Reduce heat to low and add turkey strips.
- In a saucepan, bring cream to a slow boil and add spices. Reduce heat to simmer, and stir often.
- Cook rigatoni and drain.
- Add up to 2 tablespoons Parmesan cheese to thicken cream, if necessary.
- Fold cream into sautéed mixture.
- Top rigatoni with sauce, pecans, and fresh Parmesan.

∾ BOW TIE PASTA

Serves 4

8 ounces bow tie pasta
1/4 cup olive oil
2 cloves garlic, minced
1/2 pound skinless chicken breasts, sliced
2 cups broccoli florets
3/4 cup sliced sun-dried tomatoes (in oil)
1 teaspoon dried basil
1/4 teaspoon red pepper flakes

1/4 cup white wine
3/4 cup chicken broth
1 tablespoon butter (optional)
Freshly grated Parmesan cheese

- Cook pasta according to package directions. Set aside
- Sauté minced garlic in olive oil in a large skillet or wok.
- Add sliced chicken to garlic and oil; cook until it is nearly done.
- Add broccoli and sauté for 5 minutes, stirring often.
- Add tomatoes, basil, pepper flakes, wine, broth, and butter to the mixture and simmer for 5 minutes. The broccoli should be tender crisp.
- Toss in pasta, and stir until pasta is coated and heated thoroughly.
- Serve topped with grated Parmesan.

❧ KUGEL

Serves 12

1 pound wide egg noodles
1 cup butter
1 cup sugar
12 ounces cream cheese, softened
2 cups sour cream
6 large eggs
2 cups corn flake crumbs
1 cup sliced almonds

- Boil noodles for 10 minutes or until al denté; do not use salt. Drain and set aside.
- In a large bowl, blend cream cheese, 3/4 cup butter, and 3/4 cup sugar.
- Add sour cream and eggs.
- Add noodles to mixture.
- Spread in a 12 x 10 x 2–inch greased baking dish.
- Sprinkle corn flake crumbs on top of the mixture; add almonds, and 1/4 cup sugar.
- Melt remaining 1/4 cup of butter and drizzle over all.
- Cover and refrigerate for 24 hours.
- Bake at 350° for 1 hour.

Our only recipe contributed by a Birmingham restaurant in this section on pasta and rice has some stiff competition in these two popular and delicious categories. But it stands at the top of our list for best recipes. Wild Mushroom Risotto comes to us from Bottega Restaurant and Bottega Café on Highland Avenue on Southside. These two neighboring restaurants, owned by Frances and Frank Stitt, have only been open a short time, but are among Birmingham's most popular and the Southeast's finest.

142

❧ WILD MUSHROOM RISOTTO

Serves 8 to 10

1/4 cup dried mushrooms
1/2 cup warm water
1/2 pound fresh mushrooms, shitake, crimini, or porcini
7 tablespoons butter, divided
2 teaspoons olive oil
1 onion, finely sliced
1 garlic clove, crushed
1 bay leaf
Pinch thyme
1 cup Arborio rice (or Risotto)
1/4 cup white wine
2 cups chicken broth
Salt and Pepper to taste
Freshly grated Parmesan cheese (Parmigiano-Reggiano is best)
Sprigs of fresh thyme

- Soak dried mushrooms in 1/2 cup warm water for 30 minutes; squeeze dry and reserve liquid.
- Sauté fresh mushrooms in 2 tablespoons butter.
- Heat 3 tablespoons butter and olive oil in a large pot.
- Add onion; sauté until soft about 10 minutes.
- Add garlic, bay leaf, thyme, rice, and dried mushrooms. Stir until rice is coated and shiny.
- Add wine and reserved mushroom liquid. Stir constantly until liquid is absorbed.
- Add broth 1/2 cup at a time, adding more only after the previous amount has been incorporated. A creamy emulsion will begin to form. Continue adding liquid until the rice is no longer hard, but still al dente.
- Season with salt and pepper. Add the fresh mushrooms, and beat in the last 2 tablespoons butter.

Serve with freshly grated Parmesan and garnish with sprigs of thyme.

❧ BLACK BEANS AND RICE

Serves 4 to 6

1 pound dried black beans
1 1/2 to 2 pounds smoked sausage
1 large onion, chopped
1 large bell pepper, chopped
1 cup chopped celery
3 cups cooked white rice
2 cups [8 ounces] grated medium Cheddar cheese
1 cup sour cream
Salt and pepper to taste

- Cover beans with water, and soak overnight.
- Drain and discard water.
- Place beans in a large pot and cover with fresh cold water.
- Cut sausage into bite-size pieces and brown well in a frying pan. Add to beans.
- In the same frying pan, brown onion, bell pepper, and celery.
- Add a little water to deglaze the pan, and pour all into the large pot with the beans and sausage.
- Cover and cook well for several hours, until beans are tender. Do not let water boil out.
- Serve over hot rice, sprinkle liberally with grated cheese, and top with a large dollop of sour cream.

143

⤳ RED BEANS AND RICE

Serves 6 to 8

1 pound red kidney beans
2 quarts water
1 large onion, chopped
1 bell pepper, chopped
1 bunch of green onions, chopped
3 bay leaves
1/4 teaspoon thyme
2 cloves garlic, minced
1 ham bone (optional)
1 tablespoon salt
1 teaspoon black pepper
1/4 teaspoon cayenne pepper
2 tablespoons minced parsley
1 pound Kielbasa or sausage
6 to 8 cups hot cooked rice

- Soak beans overnight in enough water to cover.
- Drain and wash beans and put them in a heavy soup pot with 2 quarts of water.
- Bring water to a boil and turn down to a simmer. Continue simmering for 1 hour.
- Add all remaining ingredients except the sausage and cooked rice. Simmer for another hour and a half or so, or until the beans have become tender and have made their own thick sauce.
- Stir occasionally to prevent scorching on the bottom. Adjust seasoning.
- Serve over hot cooked rice.

144

☙ HASHWEE
Dirty Rice
Serves 5 to 6

1 [3 pound] frying chicken
2 ribs celery, cut in thirds
1 medium onion, quartered
Salt to taste
Water to cover chicken
1/4 cup butter or margarine
1 pound ground beef
1 1/2 teaspoons salt
1/4 teaspoon pepper
1 1/2 teaspoons cinnamon
2 cups chicken broth
1 cup uncooked white rice
Pine nuts (optional)

• Wash chicken and stuff cavity with onion and celery.
• In a cooking pot, cover chicken with water and add salt.
• Bring to a boil, then lower the heat to simmer and cook for 1 hour.
• Cool chicken; skin, debone, and tear meat into large pieces.
• Return meat to pan, cover with chicken broth and set aside.
• In a large skillet, sauté ground beef and crumble until it is fine.
• Add salt, pepper, cinnamon, and butter, and sauté mixture until it is very brown.
• Add rice, chicken, and chicken broth.
• Bring to a boil, lower the heat, cover, and cook until the liquid is absorbed.
• Sauté the pine nuts in a small amount of butter, until brown.
• Serve over rice, garnished with pine nuts.

This is an unusual dish and extremely tasty.

145

 **CASSEROLE GREEN RICE**

Serves 6

1 cup uncooked white rice
1 cup milk
1 egg, beaten
1/2 teaspoon salt
1/2 cup finely chopped parsley
1/2 cup finely chopped green pepper
1 cup [4 ounces] grated Cheddar cheese
1/2 clove garlic, minced
1/4 cup salad oil

- Cook rice according to package directions.
- Add milk to beaten egg, and beat lightly to blend.
- Stir in remaining ingredients.
- Combine with rice.
- Pour into a greased 2–quart casserole.
- Bake at 350° for 45 minutes.

Delicious with beef or chicken.

HERBED RICE

Serves 6

1/4 cup butter
1 cup uncooked white rice
2 cups chicken broth
3 tablespoons instant minced onion
1/2 teaspoon rosemary
1/2 teaspoon marjoram
1/2 teaspoon thyme
1 teaspoon salt

- Combine all ingredients in a saucepan.
- Heat to boiling, stirring once.
- Cover and simmer for 20 minutes, or until rice is tender.

Headdress for Epa masquerade, African, Nigeria, Ekiti, Osi-Ilorin area, Yoruba people, twentieth century. Wood and pigment, 50 x 20 x 18 inches. Museum purchase with funds from the Birmingham City Council, Mr. and Mrs. Henry Goodrich, SONAT, Inc., Mr. and Mrs. J. Mason Davis, Beta Kappa Boule, and others.

The purpose of the Epa festival of the Yoruba is to honor ancestral culture heroes, who are considered to play an active role in the lives of their descendants. In the Epa festival, enormous helmet masks with figurative superstructures weighing up to sixty pounds are worn. The Epa ceremony often requires the wearer of the mask to dance and jump about vigorously. His success at maintaining his balance is considered a good omen for the community.

147

Andrea Simpson Garrett was an assistant in the Charles B. Hanson, Jr., Library and maintains her close ties to the museum. While she loves gourmet food, she admits that it must qualify as quick and easy before she will cook it herself. This recipe fits both qualifications and is healthy, delicious, and versatile as well.

❧ ANDREA'S PEASANT PILAF

Serves 6 to 8

1 1/2 cups uncooked white rice
6 tablespoons butter
1 cup shredded carrots
1 cup diced celery
Pepper to taste
2 tablespoons minced onion
2 tablespoons minced parsley
3 cups chicken broth
Seasoned salt to taste

- Melt 4 tablespoons of butter in a large skillet. Add rice and sauté gently, stirring frequently, for 5 minutes.
- Add remaining ingredients, except for 2 tablespoons of butter, and stir.
- Bring to a boil, cover, reduce heat, and simmer for 25 minutes.
- Add the remaining butter, stir, and serve.

For variations: summer squash, zucchini, or tomatoes may be substituted for celery and carrots. A handful of cooked, cleaned shrimp or diced chicken when you add the last of the butter makes a nice addition. Just cover and let stand off of the heat for a few minutes.

148

This recipe has a romantic past. It comes from the museum's exhibit designer, Terry Beckham, and dates back to his lean student days when the most prevalent food concern was low cost. He stir fried most of his meals and made up recipes according to the ingredients available in the cupboard. This one became a favorite and was part of the first meal he cooked for his future wife, Lynn. He credits the recipe with winning her heart. Terry insists a key to good Stir-Fried Rice is a well seasoned wok; and the bacon must not be substituted with other meats.

❧ STIR-FRIED RICE

Serves 4

1 cup uncooked white rice
4 green onions, chopped
4 slices bacon, chopped
1 [8–ounce] can water chestnuts, drained and chopped
2 eggs
Soy sauce to taste

- Cook rice according to package directions; set aside.
- Place a well-seasoned, oiled wok or large skillet on high heat.
- Cook bacon, stirring constantly.
- Just before the bacon is cooked, add onions and water chestnuts, stirring.
- Add eggs and scramble mixture together until eggs are cooked.
- Add rice and season with soy sauce to taste.

∾ BAKED RICE

Serves 6

1/2 cup butter or margarine
1 large onion, finely chopped
1 cup uncooked white rice
1 [6–ounce] can mushrooms, undrained
Pinch of salt
1 clove garlic, crushed
1/2 teaspoon oregano
1 [10 1/2–ounce] can beef consommé
1/2 can water

- Melt butter in an ovenproof skillet and brown onion lightly.
- Add rice, mushrooms with juice, salt, garlic, and oregano.
- Let mixture simmer, stirring frequently, for 20 minutes.
- Add consommé and water.
- Cover and bake at 400° for 1 hour.

∾ PECAN WILD RICE PILAF

Serves 8

1 cup wild rice, well rinsed
4 cups chicken broth
1 cup coarsley chopped pecan pieces
1 cup dried currants
1 bunch green onions, sliced
1/2 cup chopped parsley
1/2 cup chopped fresh mint or 1 tablespoon dried mint
Grated rind of 2 oranges
2 tablespoons oil (preferably olive oil)
1 tablespoon orange juice
Fresh ground pepper to taste

- Bring the chicken broth to a boil, add the wild rice, cover, and cook for 50 minutes on medium-low heat.
- Pour rice into a large bowl, add remaining ingredients, and toss.
- Serve at room temperature.

Good with turkey, duck, or quail.

149

BULGUR PILAF WITH APRICOTS AND RAISINS

Serves 4

2 teaspoons margarine
1 onion, chopped
1 cup wheat bulgur
1/4 cup raisins
1/4 cup chopped dried apricots
2 cups chicken broth
1/4 cup fresh parsley
Salt and pepper to taste

- Melt margarine and sauté onion until it is soft.
- Stir in bulgur and cook, stirring, for 1 minute.
- Stir in raisins, apricots, and broth.
- Cover and simmer over low heat for 15 minutes or until liquid is absorbed.
- Stir in parsley and salt and pepper to taste.

 BARLEY CASSEROLE

Serves 6 to 8

1/2 cup butter
1 cup quick fine pearl barley
1 medium onion, chopped
1/2 cup slivered almonds
1 [1–ounce] package onion soup mix
2 cups chicken broth
1 [4–ounce] can sliced mushrooms, reserve liquid
1 [6–ounce] can water chestnuts, drained and sliced

- Sauté onion and barley in butter until golden.
- Add soup mix, almonds, chicken broth, mushrooms with reserved liquid, and water chestnuts; stir to mix.
- Place in 2–quart casserole, cover, and bake at 350° for 1 hour. Add more liquid, if needed.

Can be prepared ahead and stored in refrigerator and reheated. Freezes well.

VEGETABLES

(Page 151) Catherine the Great of Russia Dinner Platter, *Ditchley Park, Oxfordshire,* 1773–74. Cream ware with monochrome mulberry and green enamel overglaze decoration, 19 3/8 x 14 7/8 inches. Gift of Dwight and Lucille Beeson.

In 1773 and 1774 Josiah Wedgwood devoted himself to what was perhaps his most famous and ambitious endeavor, the creation of a dinner and dessert service for fifty for Catherine the Great, Empress of Russia. Since the empress was entranced with the Western world, and particularly with British life, Wedgwood's proposal of views of England, Scotland, and Wales as the decoration for this service was warmly received. The service was to be used at Chesmenski Palace, on the outskirts of St. Petersburg, which had been built near a frog swamp. Therefore the frog crest was used on all the pieces and it came to be known as the Frog Service.
The Birmingham Museum of Art has the largest collection of eighteenth century Wedgwood outside of England, which includes three pieces from the Catherine the Great Frog Service.

VEGETABLES

❧ TO MAKE AN ARTICHOAK PYE

Take the bottoms, when boiled, of as many artichoaks as you want for your dish [*two 16–ounce cans artichoke hearts, or one can artichoke hearts and 1 can artichoke bottoms*]; season them with beaten mace, pepper and salt [*to taste*], sheet with puff paste, and lay some fresh butter at the bottom [*we suggest using a top crust only with no butter at the bottom (puff pastry recipe p. 78)*]; then lay a layer of artichoaks broke in bits, and some more butter [*1 tablespoon*] over the artichoaks; boil half an ounce of morels and truffles, strain off the water they were boiled in, cut them small, and strew them over [*if you can't get truffles and morels, use 6 to 8 button mushrooms, sautéed in 2 tablespoons butter, reserving the liquid in the pan*]; then lay another layer of artichoaks seasoned as above, and the yolks of eight or ten eggs boiled hard [*unless you love egg yolks, 3 to 4 chopped hard-cooked yolks will be sufficient*]; put a gill of white wine [*1/2 cup*] to the liquor your morels were boiled in [*or the liquid left in the pan you sautéed your mushrooms in*], and pour over the pye, lid it over, and when the crust is done, the pye will be enough. [*Bake at 350° for 40 minutes, or until the crust is golden.*]

As with the section on pasta and rice, we received an extensive and delicious selection of vegetable recipes from our members. Therefore, we have included only one additional vegetable recipe, from *The Modern Art of Cookery*. This unusual recipe is reproduced in its original form, but we have also included updated instructions in brackets for those who would like to try it. It is superb!

❧ APPLE-CRANBERRY CASSEROLE

Serves 8 to 10

3 cups chopped, unpeeled cooking apples (about 3 medium)
2 cups fresh cranberries
3/4 to 1 cup sugar
1 1/2 cups quick-cooking oats, uncooked
1/2 cup brown sugar
1/3 cup all-purpose flour
1/2 cup chopped pecans
1/2 cup margarine or butter, melted

• In a 2–quart casserole dish coated with cooking spray, combine apples, cranberries, and sugar.
• Combine remaining ingredients and add to top of casserole.
• Bake at 350° for 1 hour, or until bubbly and lightly browned.
• Serve hot.

A marvelous side dish with turkey or ham

❧ FRESH GREEN BEANS, TOMATO, AND SAVORY

Serves 4 to 6

3/4 pound fresh green beans
1 medium Vidalia or yellow onion, chopped
1 small clove garlic, pressed
1 large ripe tomato, cut into medium-size pieces
1 tablespoon olive oil
1/2 teaspoon dried Herbs de Provence or 1 teaspoon of your favorite fresh herbs
Salt and pepper to taste

- Trim and wash the green beans.
- Place enough water in a large skillet to cover the bottom. Add green beans, cover, and simmer for 10 minutes.
- Drain beans and wipe skillet dry. Add olive oil to skillet and sauté onion and garlic.
- Add green beans, tomato, herbs, salt, and pepper.
- Cook, uncovered, for about 5 minutes, until all the vegetables are tender.

❧ BROCCOLI AND RICE CASSEROLE

Serves 8

1 [10–ounce] package frozen chopped broccoli
1 [10 1/2–ounce] can cheese soup
1 [6–ounce] roll garlic cheese
2 cups cooked rice
1 [6–ounce] can chopped mushrooms
1 [2.8–ounce] can onion rings (optional)
Slivered almonds for garnish

- Prepare broccoli according to package directions.
- In a saucepan, heat soup and roll of garlic cheese together.
- Mix rice, cooked broccoli, and mushrooms with cheese.
- Place in a 2–quart casserole.
- Bake, uncovered, at 350° for 15 minutes.
- Remove from oven and top with onion rings and almonds; bake an additional 10 minutes.

❦ BRUSSELS SPROUTS WITH PARMESAN

Serves 4

1 quart Brussels sprouts
1/4 cup butter
1 large clove garlic, minced
3/4 cup chicken broth
1/2 cup freshly grated Parmesan cheese

- Clean sprouts and cut them in half lengthwise.
- Sauté with garlic in melted butter.
- Add broth and cook about 10 minutes, until almost dry and tender.
- Add cheese, let it melt, and serve immediately.

❦ A-MAIZING TOMATO BASKETS

Serves 6

6 medium fresh tomatoes
3 cups frozen corn with red and green peppers
1/2 cup chopped green onion
1/4 cup water
2 teaspoons dried summer basil
1/2 teaspoon butter flavor sprinkles
1/4 teaspoon pepper
1/2 cup shredded mozzarella cheese

- Cut tops off washed tomatoes. Gently remove pulp, leaving a "basket". Save pulp for other use.
- Combine corn, onion, and water in non-stick meduim-size skillet and cook, uncovered, on medium heat for 3 to 5 minutes, until water is absorbed and vegetables are just tender.
- Remove from heat and stir in butter sprinkles, basil, and pepper.
- Spoon mixture into tomato baskets, and top each stuffed tomato with mozzarella cheese.
- Wrap tomatoes in a cooking pouch made from heavy-duty foil; seal edges tightly. Place on upper rack of hot grill and cook 5 to 10 minutes, just until heated through. Be careful not to overcook.

This recipe was developed by Mrs. Percy Brower's cook, Robert Moffett. It offers an interesting combination of flavors.

155

❧ SHOEPEG AND BEAN CASSEROLE

Serves 6 to 8

1 [16–ounce] can French-cut green beans, drained
1 [11–ounce] can shoepeg corn, drained
1/2 cup grated sharp Cheddar cheese
1/4 cup finely chopped celery
1/4 cup finely chopped green pepper
2 tablespoons finely chopped onion
1/4 cup mayonnaise
Approximately 1 cup buttered bread crumbs

- Mix all ingredients together except bread crumbs.
- Place in a 2–quart casserole.
- Top with buttered bread crumbs.
- Bake at 350° for 20 minutes.

❧ EGGPLANT AND TOMATO PIE

Serves 8 to 10

1 9–inch unbaked pie crust
2 tablespoons grated Parmesan cheese
1 large eggplant, sliced and sautéed
4 or 5 tomatoes, sliced
1 medium to large onion, sliced into rings
1 or 2 green peppers, sliced into rings
1/2 teaspoon minced garlic
1/4 cup olive oil
Salt and pepper to taste
2 tablespoons grated Parmesan cheese

- Sprinkle pie crust with 2 tablespoons Parmesan cheese.
- Fill crust with alternate layers of sautéed eggplant, tomato, onion, and pepper.
- Sprinkle top with garlic, olive oil, salt and pepper to taste, and more Parmesan.
- Bake at 350° for 40 to 45 minutes, until vegetables are tender and crust is golden brown.
- Cut in wedges to serve.

CREOLE STUFFED EGGPLANT

Serves 4 to 5

2 small or 1 large eggplant
3/4 cup chopped onion
1/2 cup chopped green pepper
2 cloves garlic, minced
1/2 cup chopped parsley
2 tablespoons butter or margarine
2 bay leaves
1 1/2 teaspoons salt
1/2 teaspoon pepper
1/2 teaspoon crushed thyme
1 cup canned tomatoes
2/3 cup water
1 cup deveined, raw shrimp
3/4 cup bread crumbs
3 tablespoons margarine, melted

- Wash the eggplant and cut it in half lengthwise.
- Scoop out pulp and place shells upside down in a pan of cold water to prevent discoloration.
- Sauté onion, green pepper, garlic, and parsley in 2 tablespoons butter or margarine.
- Chop pulp and add to sautéed mixture.
- Add canned tomatoes, seasonings, and water.
- Cover and cook over low heat for 20 minutes or until tender.
- Remove bay leaves and add shrimp to mixture.
- Mix bread crumbs and melted margarine together.
- Fill eggplant shells with alternating layers of the shrimp mixture and crumbs.
- Place shells in a baking pan and add a small amount of water to prevent sticking.
- Bake at 400° for 40 minutes.

157

∼ LENTILS WITH ONION AND CELERY

Serves 4

1 tablespoon oil or margarine
2 onions, chopped
2 ribs celery, chopped
2 cups cooked lentils
Pinch of oregano
Salt and pepper to taste
1/2 cup fresh parsley

- Melt margarine in a large saucepan; cook onion and celery until soft.
- Add lentils and oregano.
- Cook to heat through.
- Season with salt and pepper; sprinkle with fresh parsley.

Note: 1 cup dried lentils equals 2 1/2 cups cooked.

∼ MUSHROOMS FLORENTINE

Serves 8

2 [10–ounce] packages frozen chopped spinach
1 medium onion, finely chopped
1/2 cup butter
1 pound fresh mushrooms, sliced
Garlic salt
1 1/4 cups [5 ounces] grated Cheddar cheese
Salt and freshly ground pepper to taste

- Thaw spinach and drain well.
- Sauté chopped onion in 1/4 cup of butter until it is tender.
- Add spinach, mixing well.
- Line a 9 x 13–inch baking dish with the spinach mixture.
- Sprinkle spinach mixture with garlic salt, and top with 1/2 cup Cheddar cheese.
- Sauté mushrooms in the other half of the butter.
- Add mushrooms, salt, and pepper to the casserole, then add remaining 3/4 cup cheese.
- Bake at 350° for 20 minutes.

❧ MUSHROOM PIE

Serves 4 to 6

2 pounds fresh mushrooms
1/4 cup butter
3 tablespoons all-purpose flour
1/2 cup Madeira wine
1/2 cup cream, heated
Salt and pepper to taste
Juice of 1/2 lemon
1 sheet refrigerated pie crust, cut into 1/2–inch strips

- Wash mushrooms and remove the stems.
- Heat mushroom caps on both sides in 1/4 cup butter.
- Arrange mushrooms in a 9–inch glass pie plate.
- To the juice left in the skillet, add flour, wine, cream, salt, pepper, and lemon juice.
- Stir until thick, then add the sauce to the mushrooms.
- Lay the pie crust in a basket weave design over the mushrooms.
- Bake at 450° for 15 minutes.
- Reduce oven to 350° and bake 15 minutes more.

If you wish to double this recipe, use a 9 x 13–inch pan.
Delicious with tenderloin, steaks, game, or lamb

❧ TART PEAS WITH ALMONDS

159

Serves 4

1 [10–ounce package] frozen tiny peas
2 tablespoons sour cream
Salt and pepper to taste
Toasted almonds for garnish

- Cook peas according to package directions.
- Drain well.
- Add sour cream, salt, and pepper.
- Sprinkle with toasted almonds and serve.

 PINEAPPLE CASSEROLE

Serves 8

1 [20–ounce] can pineapple chunks
1/4 cup butter or margarine
1/4 cup sugar
3 tablespoons all-purpose flour
3 tablespoons pineapple juice
1 cup [4 ounces] shredded Cheddar cheese
1 cup round buttered cracker crumbs

- Combine pineapple, butter, sugar, flour, pineapple juice, and cheese. Mix well.
- Place in a 1 1/2–quart casserole; top with cracker crumbs.
- Bake for 30 minutes at 350°.

Delicious with ham.

ROASTED NEW POTATOES WITH GARLIC

Serves 6 to 8

2 large cloves garlic, minced
1/3 cup virgin olive oil
1 1/2 pounds small new potatoes
Salt and pepper to taste
2 to 3 tablespoons chopped parsley

- Let garlic stand in olive oil overnight. Strain garlic out of oil.
- Wash potatoes well, dry, and cut in quarters. Place on a non-stick baking pan and pour oil over potatoes. Salt and pepper to taste.
- Bake at 350° about 30 minutes, until lightly browned and tender.
- Place in serving dish, sprinkle with chopped parsley, and serve.

⟨◦⟩ ROQUEFORT POTATOES AU GRATIN

Serves 6 to 8

3 to 4 Idaho potatoes, scrubbed and very thinly sliced
  (use food processor for best results)
1/4 cup butter, divided
Salt and pepper to taste
3/4 cup heavy cream
1/4 cup milk
2 ounces Roquefort cheese, crumbled
2 tablespoons plain or seasoned bread crumbs

- Grease a 2–quart square baking dish with 1 tablespoon of butter or with cooking spray.
- Arrange potatoes in layered rows.
- Sprinkle with salt and pepper and dot with 1 1/2 tablespoons butter.
- Bring cream and milk to a boil in a large non-metallic sauce pan.
- Stir in cheese and cook, stirring, until cheese melts.
- Season with salt and pepper.
- Pour mixture over potatoes.
- Cover tightly with aluminum foil.
- Bake at 425° for 1 hour 15 minutes. Check for doneness, and bake 15 minutes more if necessary.
- Uncover, sprinkle with bread crumbs, and dot with remaining butter pieces.
- Broil until potatoes are golden brown on top.
- Let stand for 10 minutes before cutting into squares.

❧ SPANAKOPITA

Serves 8 to 12

1 large onion, chopped
1 tablespoon olive oil
1 [10–ounce] package chopped spinach, squeezed dry
1/2 pound feta cheese, drained and crumbled
1/2 cup pine nuts
3 tablespoons parsley
3 tablespoons dill
Salt and pepper to taste
1/2 package frozen filo pastry, thawed
1/4 cup melted butter

• Sauté onion in oil until transparent.
• Add spinach and simmer until moisture is gone.
• Add feta, pine nuts, and seasonings.
• Brush a 9–inch pie plate with butter or olive oil.
• Working quickly to keep the filo moist, line pie plate with two layers of filo
  pastry, brush with butter, and repeat until 10 to 12 layers hang over the edge.
• Add spinach mixture.
• Top with 10 or more layers of filo, brushing with butter after every two layers.
• Fold edges toward center.
• Bake at 350° for 40 minutes or until golden brown.
• Cut in wedges to serve.

A 9 x 12–inch baking dish may be substituted for the pie plate.

❧ SPINACH ARTICHOKE CASSEROLE

Serves 6 to 8

2 [10–ounce] packages frozen chopped spinach
1 [14–ounce] can artichokes, drained (not packed in oil)
1/2 cup melted margarine
1 [8–ounce] package cream cheese, softened
1 tablespoon lemon juice
1 cup cracker crumbs
1/4 cup butter

- Cook spinach according to package directions, drain well.
- Mix margarine, cream cheese, and lemon juice together until mixture is smooth, then mix with spinach.
- Place artichokes on the bottom of a well-greased 2–quart casserole dish.
- Cover with spinach mixture, top with cracker crumbs, and dot with butter.
- Bake at 350° for 25 minutes.

Freezes very well

❧ SQUASH STUFFED WITH SPINACH

Serves 6

6 medium-size yellow crook-neck squash
1 [10–ounce] package frozen chopped spinach
Juice of 1 lemon or lime
2 tablespons margarine
1/3 cup Parmesan cheese
1/4 cup seasoned dry bread crumbs
1/4 cup cream
Salt and pepper to taste
Additional 1/2 cup Parmesan and 1/4 cup melted margarine for topping
Pimento strips for garnish

- Wash and steam whole squash for 3 to 4 minutes.
- Run them under cold water and slice off the stems and tips.
- Cut squash in half lengthwise and carefully scoop out seeds to make boats.
- Place halves in a lightly-greased 9 x 12–inch baking dish.
- Meanwhile, cook spinach until it is separated, then drain.
- Return pot of spinach to low heat; add lemon juice, margarine, salt, and pepper and stir.
- Stir in Parmesan and bread crumbs; mixture will be thick.
- Stir in cream.
- Spoon mixture into squash boats.
- Sprinkle tops with Parmesan, and drizzle with melted margarine.
- Bake at 400° for 25 to 30 minutes.
- Garnish with pimento strips.

Wonderful for a buffet
Good make-ahead dish

Michelle Luria, Volunteer Coordinator at the museum, submitted this recipe for Squash Stuffed with Spinach. It is easy to make although a bit time consuming. However, it is worth the effort. As a colorful and attractive dish, it is great for buffets or dinner parties and goes well with any meat.

163

∾ SUMMER SQUASH CASSEROLE

Serves 4 to 6

6 cups sliced yellow squash, about 2 pounds
1/4 cup chopped onion
1 [10 1/2–ounce] can condensed cream of chicken soup
1 cup sour cream
1 cup shredded carrots
1 [8–ounce] package herb seasoned stuffing mix
1/2 cup melted butter

- Cook squash and onion in boiling salted water for 5 minutes. Drain.
- In a bowl, combine soup and sour cream, and stir in carrots.
- Fold in drained squash and onions.
- In a separate bowl, combine stuffing mix and butter.
- Spread one-half of stuffing mix in the bottom of greased 2–quart baking dish.
- Spoon vegetable mixture on top.
- Sprinkle remaining stuffing mix on top.
- Bake at 350° for 30 minutes.

Zucchini may be substituted for yellow squash, if desired.

∾ SWEET POTATO DELIGHT

Serves 6 to 8

2 cups pared and grated raw sweet potatoes
2 eggs, beaten
1 cup sugar
1 cup evaporated milk or half-and-half
1/2 teaspoon cinnamon
1/2 teaspoon grated lemon rind
Dash nutmeg

- Add beaten eggs to grated potatoes and mix well.
- Gradually add sugar, milk, and butter.
- Add seasonings and mix well.
- Pour into a greased 2–quart casserole.
- Bake at 350° for 30 minutes.
- Stir casserole with a spoon and return to oven.
- Bake 15 minutes longer.

～ SWEET POTATO CASSEROLE

Serves 8

3 cups mashed sweet potatoes
1 cup sugar
2 eggs, beaten
1 teaspoon vanilla
1/2 cup melted butter or margarine
1 [3 1/2–ounce] can coconut

Topping
1/2 cup melted butter or margarine
1 cup brown sugar
1/2 cup all-purpose flour
1 cup chopped nuts

- Mix all ingredients together, except topping.
- Pour into a 2–quart casserole dish.
- Bake at 350° for 20 minutes.
- Mix all topping ingredients together and spread topping on casserole.
- Return to oven and bake until crusty, about 30 more minutes.

TOMATOES ROCKEFELLER

Serves 12

3 or 4 large tomatoes, cut into very thick slices
2 [10–ounce] packages frozen spinach, cooked, drained, and squeezed
1 cup soft bread crumbs
1 cup dry seasoned bread crumbs
6 eggs, lightly beaten
1 cup finely chopped green onions
1/2 cup grated Parmesan cheese
3/4 cup melted butter
1/2 teaspoon minced garlic
1 teaspoon salt
1 teaspoon thyme

• Arrange tomato slices in a lightly-greased 9 x 13–inch baking dish.
• Mix all other ingredients well.
• Spoon over tomatoes.
• Bake at 350° for 15 minutes or until the mixture is set.

Can be prepared a day ahead, but do not freeze.

ZUCCHINI SAUTÉ

Serves 6

2 tablespoons oil
1 small onion, finely chopped
2 or 3 medium zucchini, grated
1/2 cup cream or milk
2/3 cup grated Swiss cheese
Salt and pepper to taste

• Sauté onions in oil in a large skillet.
• Add zucchini and toss in the pan for 2 to 3 minutes, until it is almost cooked through.
• Add cream; mix thoroughly.
• Add cheese, mixing well, and simmer for 3 minutes.
• Add salt and pepper and serve.

❧ BAKED VEGETABLES WITH HERBS

Serves 6 to 8

5 red potatoes, sliced thin with skin on
1/2 [9–ounce] package frozen Italian green beans
1 medium zucchini, sliced
1 medium yellow squash, sliced
1 bunch spring onions, sliced
1/2 pound fresh mushrooms, sliced
1 pint cherry tomatoes
Salt and pepper to taste
Oregano or basil

Marinade

1/4 cup olive oil
1/4 cup wine
1/4 cup basalmic vinegar
Juice of 1/2 lemon
1 tablespoon sweet pickle juice
1/2 teaspoon sugar, if needed

- Layer all the vegetables, except the cherry tomatoes, in a 4–quart baking dish.
- Sprinkle with salt, pepper, and oregano or basil.
- Mix marinade ingredients well and pour over vegetables.
- Cut tomatoes in half; placing the cut side down, layer on top of the vegetables, covering top completely.
- Cover lightly with foil.
- Bake at 350° for 2 hours.

VEGETABLE CASSEROLE

Serves 10

1 1/2 cups chopped onion
1 1/2 cups chopped carrots
2 cups chopped celery
1/2 green pepper, chopped
2 cups canned tomatoes, well drained
1 tablespoon sugar
2 teaspoons seasoned salt
3 tablespoons tapioca
1/4 cup melted margarine
1 [10–ounce] package frozen sliced green beans, thawed

- Mix all ingredients together, except green beans.
- Place in a 9 x 12–inch casserole dish.
- Bake, uncovered, at 350° for 1 hour.
- Layer green beans on top of other vegetables, cover, and bake for an additional 30 to 45 minutes.

SALADS & DRESSINGS

(Page 169) Attributted to Hubert van Ravesteyn (Dutch, 1638–91), *Kitchen Interior*, mid-seventeenth century. Oil on canvas, 32 1/2 x 26 3/8 inches. Museum purchase with funds from the 1976 and 1977 Beaux Arts Committee.

Seventeenth-century Dutch art was a phenomenon unlike any other in European art at the time. Its roots were in the Reformation and an economy built on commerce which gave rise to a new art market, the middle class merchant with extra cash to spend on the finer things in life. One of these was fine art. While the rest of European painting still concentrated on portraiture and religious and classical subjects, Dutch art reflected an interest in everyday life and consisted of genre scenes, landscapes, and still life paintings. *Kitchen Interior* is an excellent example of seventeenth-century Dutch genre painting, marked by its careful draughtsmanship and attention to detail as well as the use of chiaroscuro, heavy contrasts of light and dark.

SALADS

KING RICHARD'S SALAT

Take parsel, sawge, garlec, chibollas, onyons, leeks, borage, myntes, fenel, and ton tressis, rew, rosemarye, purslayre. Lave, and waishe hem clene; pike hem, pluk hem small with thyn hande and myng hem wel with rawe oile. Lat one vynegar and salt, and serve it forth.

[*Take parsley, sage, garlic, small onions, onions, leeks, borage, mint, fennel, cress, rue, rosemary, purslane. Rinse and wash them clean; pick them over, tear them with your hands and mix them well with oil. Add vinegar and salt, and serve it forth.*]

TO MAKE A GRAND SALLET FOR SPRING

Your gardiner, or those that serve you with herbs, must supply you with all manner of Spring-Sallets, as buds of Cowslips, Violets, Stawberries, Primrose, Brooklime, Watercresses, young Lettice, Spinnage, Alexanderbuds, or what other things may be got. Then take Sampier, Olives, Capers, Broom-buds, Cowcumbers, Raisons and Currans parboyled, blanched Almonds, Barberries, or what other pickles you can obtain. Then prepare your standard for the middle of your dish; it may be a wax tree or a castle made of paste, washed in the yolks of eggs and all made greene with herbs and stuck with flowers, with about twelve supporters fastened in holes in your Castle and bending out to the middle of your dish. Then having four rings of paste, one bigger than another, place them so they rise like so many steps. This done, place your Sallet, a round of one sort on the uppermost ring and so round the others till you come to the dish; then place all your pickles from that to the brim and place the colors white against white and green against the green. Garnish your dish with all things suitable or afforded by the Spring. Your statutes ought to have Cruitts placed in their hands, two with Vinegar and two with Oyl, sized over on the outside and strowed with flowers.

When this Sallet is made, let it be carried to the Table, and when the guests are placed, unstop the Cruitts, that the Oyl and Vinegar may run on the Sallet. After the same manner may you make your Sallet in Summer, Autumn or Winter; only take those Sallets that are then in season, and change your Standard: in Summer you ought to resemble a green tree; in Autumn a castle carved out of Carrets and Turnips; in the Winter, a tree hanged with Snow. This is only for Great Feasts, and we may inform the Practitioner for the honour of his Master and benefit of himself: the Paste that you make your Castle or Standard with, must be made of Rye.

We open the section on salads with two superbly entertaining recipes from *The Delectable Past*. The first is from *The Forme of Cury* published in 1390 in England for the staff of Richard II, a monarch who apparently loved good food as much as he loved the crown. This salad is surprisingly contemporary and shows that some recipes are so delicious it is futile to try to improve them. We suggest using your favorite salad greens with olive oil and herb or wine vinegar, to your taste. The second salad recipe is also English and is from a cookbook by William Rabisha published in 1661 and titled *The Whole Body of Cookery Dissected, Taught, and fully manifested, Methodically, Artificially, and according to the best Tradition of English, French, Italian, Dutch , &c*. The recipe is as elaborate as the title of the cookbook, and will be attempted by only the most flamboyant of hosts, or those in whose employ the Practitioner will perform "for the honour of his Master and benefit of himself."

171

Babbie Shelton, past president of the members board, has shared with us a recipe she improvised. This versatile dish is wonderful to serve at a luncheon since it goes a long way and is absolutely delicious.

172

❧ TANGY RICE AND CHICKEN SALAD

Serves 4 to 6

4 boneless, skinless chicken breasts
Water to cover chicken
Salt and pepper to taste
1 1/2 cups white rice
3 1/4 cups chicken stock or canned broth
4 green onions, cut into thin slices
1/2 green pepper, chopped
12 pimento-stuffed olives, sliced
1 [12–ounce] jar marinated artichoke hearts, quartered (reserve marinade)
1 teaspoon curry powder
1 1/2 tablespoons olive oil
1 1/2 tablespoons vinegar
2/3 cups mayonnaise

- In a shallow pan, place chicken breasts with enough water to cover, and salt and pepper to taste.
- Cover, bring slowly to a boil, and simmer until done, about 25 to 30 minutes.
- Drain and set aside to cool.
- Meanwhile, cook rice in stock until tender.
- Cool slightly and combine with onions, olives, green peppers, and artichokes.
- Pull chicken apart into bite-size pieces.
- Combine the reserve marinade with the mayonnaise, curry powder, olive oil, and vinegar.
- Add to the rice mixture along with the chicken. Toss and chill.

Good served with fruit salad and/or chilled soup, crisp bread, or pita toast.

❧ CURRIED CHICKEN SALAD

Serves 6

2 cups diced cooked chicken
2 cups cooked rice
1/3 cup sliced green onions
1 1/2 cups cooked peas (fresh or frozen)
1 1/4 cups mayonnaise
1 1/2 teaspoons curry powder
1 teaspoon salt
1 1/4 teaspoons black pepper
1 1/2 tablespoons fresh lemon juice
2 tablespoons chopped pimento

- Combine chicken, rice, onions, and peas; set aside.
- Prepare dressing using mayonnaise, curry powder, salt, black pepper, and lemon juice.
- Pour dressing over the chicken mixture, and mix well. Fold in chopped pimentos.
- Garnish with tomatoes and cucumbers.

May be prepared ahead.

❧ CHICKEN SALAD SUPREME

Serves 4 to 6

2 1/2 cups cubed, cooked chicken breast
1 cup finely chopped celery
1/2 cup sliced toasted almonds
1 cup white seedless grapes, halved
2 tablespoons finely chopped parsley
1/2 teaspoon salt
1 cup mayonnaise
1 cup heavy cream, whipped

- Mix all ingredients together; chill.

For calorie conscious, whipped cream may be omitted.

173

Kathy G's Caterers is located on Montgomery Highway in Vestavia Hills, and is fast becoming one of the area's favorites. Salads and summer just go together in the South and Kathy G's offers two variations of this popular dish. The first is a delicious chicken salad with an Oriental flavor for a change from the ordinary.

174

ORIENTAL CHICKEN PASTA SALAD
Serves 4 to 6 as an entrée, 8 as a side dish

16 ounces medium seashell pasta
1/2 pound pea pods or fresh asparagus in season
2 cups diced boiled chicken
1 1/2 cups chopped celery
1 [8–ounce] package frozen peas
1/2 cup finely-chopped green onions
1 [8–ounce] can sliced water chestnuts
Soy-ginger dressing (recipe follows)

• Cook pasta according to package directions.
• Drain and rinse with cold water.
• Steam pea pods 1 to 2 minutes; drain.
• Combine pasta, pea pods, chicken, celery, peas, onions, and water chestnuts and toss gently.
• Pour dressing over pasta mixture and toss until well blended.

Soy Ginger Dressing
1 2/3 cups mayonnaise
2 tablespoons soy sauce
1/4 teaspoon salt
Dash white pepper
2 teaspoons ground ginger
1 tablespoon sesame oil

• Combine all ingredients and mix well.

⤳ JOE BAR'S TURKEY PASTA SALAD

Serves 6 to 10

1 [16–ounce] package frozen baby lima beans
2 pounds turkey breast, cooked and chopped
2 pounds rainbow pasta spirals, cooked and drained
4 cups [16 ounces] sharp Cheddar cheese, cubed
1 small onion, chopped
1 large bunch celery, chopped
1 cup chopped bell pepper
3 cups mayonnaise
10 ounces Durkee's famous sauce
1/2 cup leaf tarragon
4 tablespoons black pepper

- Cook pasta according to package directions; when draining, pour hot pasta water over thawed lima beans, then drain beans.
- Combine all ingredients, and chill.
- Serve cold.

Joe Bar is in its second life, having moved from Five Points South after a fire, to Seventh Avenue South in Lakeview. It is a favorite Birmingham haunt for those in the arts community, as well as many others. Their recipe for turkey pasta salad is another delightful dish that can be served on those hot summer days.

175

When you are looking for a delicious change from shrimp or chicken salads, this recipe could be the perfect choice. It was submitted by the museum's curator of decorative arts, Bryding Adams, who claims it is standard fare for her spring and summer table.

COLD STEAK SALAD

Serves 6

2 pounds boneless sirloin, cut into 1/2–inch cubes
1/2 cup butter
3/4 pound mushrooms, sliced
1 [9–ounce] package frozen artichoke hearts, cooked and cooled
1 cup finely diced celery
1 pint small cherry tomatoes
2 tablespoons chopped chives
2 tablespoons chopped parsley
2 cups salad dressing (recipe follows)

- In a large skillet over high heat, sauté meat cubes, a few at a time in butter until browned on all sides. Transfer to a large bowl and cool.
- Quickly sauté mushrooms in butter remaining in skillet and add to bowl with artichoke hearts, celery, tomatoes, chives and parsley. Add dressing, toss, cover, and marinate over night.

Dressing

Makes 3 1/2 cups

2 1/4 cups oil
3/4 cup red wine vinegar
6 shallots, finely chopped
1/3 cup chopped parsley
1/3 cup snipped fresh dill weed
Salt and freshly ground black pepper
1/8 teaspoon hot sauce
2 teaspoons Dijon mustard

- Combine everything in a glass jar and shake.

∾ MEXICAN CHEF SALAD

Serves 4 to 6

1 pound ground beef
1 [1 1/4–ounce] package dry taco seasoning mix
1/2 cup water
1 [15–ounce] can kidney beans, undrained
1 avocado, peeled and chopped
1 small head of lettuce, torn
1 onion, chopped
1 clove garlic, minced
3 to 4 tomatoes, chopped
1 [12 to 18–ounce] package tortilla chips, crushed
2 cups [8 ounces] shredded sharp Cheddar cheese

- Brown beef and drain.
- Add taco seasoning mix and 1/2 cup water, stir well and cook until beef is done.
- In a separate pan, mash kidney beans and cook until moisture is absorbed.
- Cool beef and beans while preparing salad ingredients.
- In a wooden salad bowl, lightly toss avocados, lettuce, onion, garlic, tomatoes, tortilla chips, and cheese.
- Add beef and beans, tossing gently. Serve immediately.

Variation: Add chopped green onions, black olives, and sour cream.

177

Buttiker's Café has included a wonderful salad recipe that proves it is often the simplest and least pretentious dishes that offer the best dining experiences. With just three ingredients—salad greens, grilled salmon, and lemon vinaigrette sauce—this dish is a classic.

❧ EPICUREAN GRILLED SALMON SALAD

Serves 2

8 ounces salmon cut into strips
2 to 3 cups mixed salad greens

Lemon Vinaigrette Sauce
Juice of 1/2 lemon
1/4 cup extra virgin olive oil
2 tablespoons vinegar
1 tablespoon chopped parsley
1 tablespoon chopped onion
Thyme
Oregano
Salt and pepper to taste

- Grill salmon strips and place on top of clean, dry salad greens.
- Mix remaining ingredients together well.
- Pour over salmon and salad greens and serve.

❧ FRUITED SHRIMP SALAD

Serves 6

1 pound cooked shrimp, peeled and deveined
2 cups diced fresh pears, unpeeled
2 cups diced fresh red apples, unpeeled
1 cup thinly sliced celery
1/2 cup mayonnaise or salad dressing
2 tablespoons milk
1 tablespoon cider vinegar
2 teaspoons grated onion
1 teaspoon salt
Salad greens
Paprika

- Combine shrimp, pears, apples, and celery in a large bowl.
- Blend mayonnaise, milk, vinegar, onion, and salt.
- Pour over shrimp mixture and toss lightly. Cover and chill at least 30 minutes.
- Serve on salad greens; sprinkle with paprika.

Garnish with fresh tomatoes and pickles.

ᖚ GARDEN SALAD

Serves 6

1 pound green beans cut into 1 1/2–inch lengths
1 pound wax beans cut into 1 1/2–inch lengths,
    or 2 [16–ounce] cans waxed beans, drained
1 [16–ounce] can kidney beans, drained
3 oranges cut into thin slices and quartered,
    or 2 [11–ounce] cans mandarin oranges, drained
1/2 red onion, sliced thinly
1 bunch scallions, chopped
Whites of 2 hard-cooked eggs, chopped
1 cup salad dressing (recipe follows)

• Cook green beans in boiling salted water until barely tender, about 8 minutes; drain.
• If fresh wax beans are used, cook as above. Combine green, wax, and kidney beans, orange slices, onion, and scallions.
• Add egg white to dressing and pour over beans. Toss and chill before serving.

Dressing

Makes 2 cups

1 cup olive oil
6 tablespoons white wine vinegar
3 shallots, finely chopped
3 tablespoons chopped parsley
3 tablespoons chopped fresh dill weed
Salt and freshly ground black pepper
Dash hot sauce

• Combine dressing ingredients in a covered container and shake.

179

C'est Bon has been opened for several years and is located on Highland Avenue on Southside. After starting out as a lunch spot and bakery, C'est Bon has evolved into one of the premier restaurants for evening dining in the city, serving superb food in an intimate setting. They have given us two recipes for classic salads, Caesar's Salad and Greek Salad. We include a quote from them on Greek food: "Greek food is so different and so tasty that people just love it. The spices and flavors are kind of exotic and people enjoy having something different. A Greek meal generally includes plenty of whole grains and olive oil, both of which may help lower blood cholesterol levels."
Nedva Wilson, Assistant Professor of Nutrition, University of Alabama at Birmingham

 ## CAESAR'S SALAD

Serves 6

3 to 4 small heads of Romaine lettuce, washed, trimmed, and well chilled

Dressing

2 egg yolks
4 garlic cloves, minced
1/2 teaspoon salt
4 ounces freshly grated Parmesan cheese
6 anchovy fillets, minced
1 teaspoon Worcestershire sauce
3 to 4 drops red pepper hot sauce
1/2 cup fresh lemon juice
2 tablespoons Dijon mustard
2 tablespoons minced fresh parsley
1 cup extra virgin olive oil
10 kalamata olives, pitted and minced

- Coddle egg yolks for 1 minute in a heatproof dish set in a water bath of hot but not boiling water. Stir yolks to heat through, but do not cook. If yolks begin to cook, remove from heat and hot water immediately and stir in several teaspoons of cold water.
- Combine all dressing ingredients, except oil and parsley, in a stainless steel bowl; beat with a wire whisk. Your mixture should look like a very thick paste.
- Gradually add oil and stir until well blended. Mix in parsley.
- Cover and chill dressing overnight.

Croutons

6 [1/4–inch thick] slices white bread crusts trimmed, cut into 1/4–inch cubes (such as French baguette or sour dough)
1/4 cup olive oil
2 large garlic cloves, minced
1/4 cup freshly grated Parmesan cheese
1/4 cup parsley
1/4 teaspoon salt and pepper
1 teaspoon dry oregano

- In a bowl, combine croutons with olive oil, garlic, Parmesan cheese, parsley, salt, pepper, and oregano. Toss well.
- Place bread cubes on a cookie sheet.
- Bake at 300° until slightly brown, about 10 minutes. Cool.

To assemble salad
- In a clean stainless steel bowl, combine the lettuce, cut in chunks, with the dressing. Toss in croutons and mix well.
- Serve on well chilled plates.
- Top with a little Parmesan cheese and fresh ground black pepper and serve.

It is always better to do your dressing by hand using a wooden spoon or a wire whisk instead of a food processor because the flavors of all the ingredients taste better.

⮑ GREEK SALAD

Serves 4

4 large ripe tomatoes, diced (about 1 1/2 pounds)
2 cucumbers, peeled, seeded, and cut in 1–inch cubes
4 green onions, thinly sliced
2 tablespoons minced fresh dill
2 tablespoons minced fresh parsley
2 tablespoons dry oregano
1 teaspoon salt
1 teaspoon black pepper
1/2 cup extra virgin olive oil
1/4 cup sherry wine vinegar
4 ounces imported feta cheese*
15 to 20 kalatmata olives*

- In a large bowl combine the tomatoes, cucumbers, green onions, dill, parsley, oregano, salt, and pepper.
- Toss with olive oil and vinegar and refrigerate for up to 1 hour, allowing all the flavors to blend with each other.
- Serve on chilled salad plates. Top with feta and olives.

Serve with good crusty white bread such as French baguette.

* Feta and olives are available at Italian markets and some supermarkets.

MARINATED ASPARAGUS AND HEARTS OF PALM

Serves 12

3 pounds fresh asparagus
2 [14–ounce] cans hearts of palm, drained and cut into 1/2–inch slices
1 cup vegetable oil
1/2 cup cider vinegar
3 cloves garlic, crushed
1 1/2 teaspoons salt
1 teaspoon pepper
Cherry tomatoes

- Snap off tough ends of asparagus. Remove scales from stalks with a knife.
- Place asparagus in steaming rack over boiling water; cover and steam for 4 minutes.
- Drain and submerge in ice water to cool. Drain asparagus well.
- Combine asparagus and hearts of palm in a zip-top, heavy-duty plastic bag.
- Combine oil and next four ingredients in a jar; cover tightly, and shake vigorously.
- Pour dressing over vegetables. Seal bag and marinate in refrigerator 8 hours; turn bag occasionally.
- Add tomatoes and serve.

 ITALIAN GREEN BEAN SALAD

Serves 6 to 8

2 pound green beans, trimmed
1 large red onion, thinly sliced
1 cup pine nuts, lightly toasted
Salt and fresh ground pepper to taste

Mustard Vinaigrette Dressing
1 tablespoon stone ground mustard
1 teaspoon salt
9 tablespoons olive oil
3 tablespoons balsamic vinegar

- Cook beans in salted water till crisp-tender, about 5 minutes. Drain and rinse under cold water. Drain and dry.
- Combine vinegar, mustard, and salt in a medium size bowl and slowly whisk in oil in a thin stream.
- Combine beans, onions, and 1/2 cup of pine nuts in a large bowl. Mix in the dressing and season with salt and pepper. Let marinate 15 to 45 minutes.
- Place in serving dish, sprinkle with remaining pine nuts, and serve.

❧ DELECTABLE BROCCOLI SALAD

Serves 10

3/4 cup raisins
4 to 5 cups fresh raw broccoli florets, cut into bite size pieces
8 slices bacon, cooked and crumbled
1/2 cup thinly sliced celery
1/2 cup toasted sunflower seeds

Dressing
1 cup mayonnaise
2 tablespoons balsamic vinegar
1/4 cup sugar
1 teaspoon curry powder

- Soak raisins in warm water; drain well.
- Combine raisins, broccoli florets, bacon, celery, and sunflower seeds.
- In a small bowl, make dressing by combining mayonnaise, vinegar, sugar, and curry powder.
- Just before serving, add dressing mixture to salad ingredients. Toss gently.

Ingredients may be prepared ahead and stored in the refrigerator in plastic bags. Dressing should be prepared and added just before serving.

This unusual recipe from Jim and Sue Huffer received raves when it was served at the Volunteer Council luncheon. The unexpected taste combination always prompts requests for the recipe. This recipe can be doubled or halved easily.

183

❧ BRUSSELS SPROUTS RELISH

Serves 6 to 8

2 [10–ounce] packages frozen brussels sprouts
1 small green bell pepper, chopped
1 [14–ounce] bottle Italian dressing

- Cook sprouts for 10 minutes in small amount of water. Drain well.
- In a 1–quart glass jar or glass bowl, layer sprouts, alternating with green pepper.
- Pour Italian dressing over the mixture, cover, and marinate for 8 to 10 hours in the refrigerator. Toss several times.
- Remove from refrigerator approximately 30 minutes before serving. Drain well.

Excellent with any meat.

❧ CORN SALAD

Serves 10 to 12

2 [16–ounce] packages frozen shoepeg corn, cooked and drained
1/2 medium onion, chopped
1/2 medium green pepper, chopped
1/2 medium cucumber, chopped
1/2 cup mayonnaise
1 tablespoon lemon juice
1 teaspoon sugar
1/2 teaspoon salt
1/2 teaspoon pepper
1/2 teaspoon dry mustard
1/2 teaspoon celery seeds
Paprika

- Combine vegetables in a medium-size bowl and set aside.
- In a small bowl, blend mayonnaise, lemon juice, sugar, salt, pepper, dry mustard, and celery seeds.
- Combine vegetables and dressing; toss lightly. Sprinkle with paprika and refrigerate until ready to serve.

Best when served the day it is prepared.
Variations: 6 to 8 sliced cherry tomatoes may be added just before serving.

Note: 2 [11–ounce] cans of shoepeg corn or 4 ears of fresh corn may be substituted for frozen corn.

CINNAMON PINEAPPLE CARROTS

Serves 12 to 16

1 1/2 pounds carrots
1 cup water
1/2 teaspoon salt
1 [20–ounce] can pineapple chunks, undrained
1/2 cup cider vinegar
1/2 cup sugar
1 stick cinnamon
2 whole cloves

- Pare carrots and cut them into sticks or rounds to measure about 4 1/2 cups.
- Cook carrots in salted water for about 10 minutes, until barely tender, and drain.
- Drain syrup from the pineapple into a saucepan.
- Add vinegar, sugar, cinnamon stick, and cloves.
- Heat to boiling, stirring until sugar dissolves.
- Place carrots and pineapple chunks in a serving dish.
- Pour syrup mixture over carrots and pineapple chunks.
- Cover and refrigerate overnight or longer before serving.

Can be prepared ahead and stored in refrigerator for 2 weeks.

❧ MARINATED CARROTS

Serves 12

5 cups sliced carrots (approximately 2 pounds)
1 medium onion, thinly sliced
1 medium bell pepper, thinly sliced
1 [10 1/2–ounce] can condensed tomato soup
1/2 cup vegetable oil
1 cup sugar
3/4 cup cider vinegar
1 teaspoon salt
1 teaspoon prepared mustard
1 teaspoon white or black pepper
1 teaspoon Worcestershire sauce

• Cook carrots until they are barely tender. Drain.
• Combine carrots, onions, and bell pepper in a covered glass container.
• Mix remaining ingredients together and pour over vegetables.
• Marinate in refrigerator for 12 hours or longer.

May be kept in the refrigerator for 2 weeks. This recipe improves with age.

❧ MARINATED TOMATOES

Makes 6 servings

3 large tomatoes
1/3 cup olive oil
1/4 cup red wine vinegar
1 teaspoon salt
1/4 teaspoon pepper
1/2 clove garlic, crushed
1 tabelspoon chopped parsley
1 tablespoon chopped fresh basil or 1 teaspoon dried whole basil
2 tablespoons chopped onion

• Cut tomatoes into 1/2–inch thick slices, and arrange in a large shallow dish; set aside.
• Combine remaining ingredients in a jar; cover tightly, and shake vigorously.
• Pour over tomato slices.
• Cover and marinate in refrigerator several hours.

～ CHUNKY GARDEN SALAD SALSA

Makes 3 cups

2 cups fresh chopped tomatoes, peeled and seeded; reserve juice
1/2 cup diced sweet onion
1/3 cup diced sweet yellow pepper
1 tablespoon chopped fresh parsley
1/4 cup grated Parmesan cheese
3 tablespoons balsamic vinegar
1 tablespoon canola oil
1 tablespoon chopped fresh basil
1 teaspoon sugar
1/8 teaspoon black pepper

- Place first 5 ingredients, including tomato juice, in a bowl and toss lightly.
- Combine vinegar, oil, basil, sugar, and pepper in a small bowl and blend until sugar is dissolved.
- Pour vinegar mixture over tomato mixture and toss gently until well blended.
- Let stand 30 minutes.
- Delicious alone as a chilled salad, or serve over torn mixed salad greens; also excellent tossed with cooked, chilled bow-tie pasta as a pasta salad.

187

❧ PLANTATION MEDLEY

Serves 8

1/2 cup vinegar
1/2 cup sugar
1/4 cup oil
1 1/2 teaspoons celery seeds
1 1/2 teaspoons salt
1 [16–ounce] can peas, drained
1 cup sliced celery
1 [8–ounce] can cut green beans, drained
1 [4–ounce] can mushrooms, drained
1/3 cup chopped green pepper
1/4 cup chopped onion
1 [2–ounce] jar pimento, chopped and drained

• Combine vinegar, sugar, oil, and seasonings and beat until thoroughly blended.
• Combine all the vegetables.
• Pour dressing mixture over vegetables. Mix lightly and cover.
• Marinate in refrigerator several hours or overnight.

Will keep in the refrigerator for 2 weeks.

⌒⌒ LINGUINE WITH OLIVES

Serves 8 to 10 as a side dish

1 pound linguine
1 cup sliced green olives
1 cup black olives (preferably Greek style), sliced or whole
1 red onion, finely diced
1 to 2 fresh tomatoes, diced, or 1 pint cherry tomatoes
1 medium zucchini, diced small
Olivada vinaigrette (recipe follows)

- Cook linguine according to package directions.
- Drain and rinse with cold water.
- Toss linguine with olives, onions, tomatoes, and zucchini.
- Pour on Olivada dressing and toss until well blended.

Olivada Vinaigrette

2 cloves garlic
1/2 teaspoon salt
1/4 cup white wine vinegar
1 1/2 teaspoons Italian seasoning
1/2 teaspoon pepper
2/3 cup olive oil
1 tablespoon olive paste

- With a mortar and pestle, grind garlic with salt.
- Add vinegar, Italian seasonings, and pepper.
- Whisk in olive oil.
- Add 1 tablespoon olive paste and blend in mixture.

Our second recipe from Kathy G's Catering is an unusual pasta salad with a taste of the Mediterranean. The dish is perfect for those hot summer lunches when you crave something out of the ordinary. Olive paste can be found in the condiment section of most full-line grocery stores.

189

❧ PASTA SALAD

Serves 12

1 pound uncooked vegetable rotini
1 green pepper, chopped
1 sweet red pepper, chopped
1 [8–ounce] can sliced water chestnuts, drained
1 bunch green onions, chopped
Cherry tomatoes (optional)
3/4 cup vegetable oil
1/4 cup cider vinegar
1 1/2 teaspoons salt
1 1/2 teaspoons pepper
1 clove garlic, crushed

• Cook pasta according to package directions, omitting salt; drain.
• Rinse with cold water; drain.
• In a bowl, combine pasta, peppers, water chestnuts, green onions, and, if desired, cherry tomatoes.
• Combine oil and remaning ingredients, mixing well.
• Pour over pasta mixture, stirring to coat well.
• Cover and chill 8 hours; stir occasionally.

190

∿ GRAPE AND ALMOND COLE SLAW

Serves 10 to 12

1 teaspoon salt
1 teaspoon sugar
1 teaspoon dry mustard
2 tablespoons vinegar
1 cup mayonnaise
1 medium head cabbage, finely chopped
2 cups white grapes, seedless or seeded
1 cup slivered blanched almonds
Fresh parsley

- Mix salt, sugar, mustard, and vinegar together. Blend in mayonnaise.
- Pour dressing over cabbage and toss.
- Add grapes and almonds, and toss gently.
- Serve in a wide shallow glass bowl. Arrange a wreath of fresh parsley and grapes on top.

Add cubed white meat chicken for a delightful chicken salad.

∿ 24–HOUR COLE SLAW

Serves 10

1 [3–pound] cabbage, thinly sliced
2 medium-size bell peppers, thinly sliced
2 medium white onions, thinly sliced
1 cup vinegar
1 cup vegetable oil
1 cup sugar
2 teaspoons salt
1 tablespoon dry mustard
2 teaspoons celery seeds

- Combine first 3 ingredients in a large bowl.
- Mix remaining ingredients in a small sauce pan, and bring to a boil. Pour over cabbage mixture.
- Cover and refrigerate for 24 hours.

Will keep for 7 days in refrigerator.

191

TROPICAL FRUIT COMPOTE

Serves 6

1/2 cup salad oil
3 tablespoons cider vinegar
1 tablespoon lemon juice
1/4 teaspoon salt
1 teaspoon sugar
1 medium clove garlic, pressed
1/8 teaspoon white pepper
1/4 teaspoon curry powder
1 [20–ounce] can pineapple chunks, drained
1 [11–ounce] can mandarin oranges, drained
1 small red onion, thinly sliced
1 medium avocado, peeled and chopped
1/2 cup flaked coconut

• In a medium-size bowl, whisk first 8 ingredients until well blended.
• Add pineapple, oranges, onion, and avocado; toss until well coated.
• Cover and refrigerate until well chilled.
• Before serving, sprinkle top with coconut.

Excellent as a side dish or salad. Especially good with pork.

❧ CRANBERRIES IN THE SNOW

Serves 6 to 8

1 [3–ounce] package dark cherry flavored gelatin
1 cup boiling water
1 [15 1/2–ounce] can whole-berry cranberry sauce
1/2 cup chopped celery
1/2 cup chopped pecans, lightly toasted
1 cup sour cream

- Dissolve gelatin in boiling water; refrigerate until it is partially thickened.
- Add remaining ingredients, blend well, and pour into a greased mold.
- When firm, unmold and serve with a dollop of mayonnaise on top.

❧ HOLIDAY SURPRISE

Serves 12

3 [3–ounce] packages raspberry flavored gelatin
3/4 cup boiling water
3 [15–ounce] cans plain tomatoes, undrained
2 to 4 dashes hot sauce
Sour cream
Horseradish

- Dissolve gelatin in boiling water. Cool.
- Combine gelatin mixture with tomatoes and hot sauce. Pour into individual molds and refrigerate.
- When chilled and ready to serve, unmold onto individual plates.
- Make a dressing of sour cream and horseradish to taste, and place a dollop on top of each serving.

May be prepared for 4 by reducing recipe to 1/3.

Susan Johnston brought this unique recipe back with her when returning from Alaska. The unusual combination of ingredients produces an incredibly beautiful color, perfect for a holiday meal.

193

Paul de Lamerie (French, 1688–1751), Basket, 1740–41. Silver, 9 3/4 x 11 inches. Bequest of Frances Oliver Estate.

Paul Storr (English, 1771–1844), Stand, 1820–21. Silver, 3 x 14 inches. Bequest of Frances Oliver Estate.

The complementary workmanship and design of Paul de Lamerie and Paul Storr, perhaps the foremost silversmiths working in London during the mid-eighteenth and early nineteenth centuries, can be seen in this superb rococo basket and stand. The basket was used for bread and sweetmeats, and its design reflects the rich decorative vocabulary imported by an entire generation of French silversmiths working in England in the eighteenth century. The stand was made for the basket eighty years later and reveals Storr's versatile talents. In scale, quality, and alignment, the stand appears indistinguishable as a separate piece from the basket.

194

SALAD DRESSINGS

FRENCH VINAIGRETTE DRESSING

Makes 2 1/2 cups

1 [10 1/2–ounce] can condensed tomato soup
1/2 cup oil
2/3 cup sugar
1/3 cup white vinegar
1 1/4 teaspoons brown mustard
1 1/4 teaspoons Worcestershire sauce
Salt and pepper to taste

• Mix all ingredients together well in a blender and chill.

Excellent on a garden salad

SPINACH SALAD DRESSING

Makes about 2 1/2 cups

4 slices bacon
1 egg, beaten
1/2 cup sugar
1/2 cup white wine vinegar
Dash of salt
1 [11 1/2–ounce] can mandarin orange segments, drained

• Cook bacon until crisp and set aside; reserve 1 1/2 teaspoons bacon drippings.
• In a saucepan, combine egg, sugar, vinegar, salt, and reserved bacon drippings.
• Bring to a boil, stirring often. Set aside to cool.
• Crumble reserved bacon.
• Combine cooked mixture, crumbled bacon, and orange segments.
  Add dressing to fresh spinach and toss well.

Dressing stores well in refrigerator, but should be served at room temperature.

Our first salad dressing comes from the Back Alley restaurant. Salads are an important part of their menu, and are the perfect entrée for summer outdoor dining. The restaurant makes all their own salad dressings, and this versatile French is equally delicious on salad greens, a chef's salad, a grilled meat or fish salad, or fruit.

195

Carolyn Emmons' baby sister gave this favorite dressing its unusual name when she was very small. She was inspired by its color and her fascination with fairytale dragons.

❧ DRAGON'S BLOOD SALAD DRESSING

Makes about 3 cups

1 1/2 cups ketchup
1/2 cup extra virgin olive oil
1/2 cup red wine vinegar
1/3 cup Worcestershire sauce
1/4 cup honey
1 tablespoon garlic powder

• Whisk ingredients together until well blended.
• Chill and serve.

Great on all salad greens.
Makes a great fruit salad dressing with the addition of poppy seeds or sliced almonds.

❧ THOUSAND ISLAND DRESSING WITH CHEESE

Makes about 1 1/2 cups

1/2 cup buttermilk
1/2 cup mayonnaise
3 tablespoons ketchup
2 tablespoons sugar
1/4 teaspoon each: salt, red pepper, paprika, garlic powder, and black pepper
2 large carrots, chopped
1 medium onion, chopped
4 tablespoons grated Parmesan or crumbled Roquefort cheese

• Combine all ingredients except cheese in a blender container.
  Cover and blend until the mixture is smooth.
• Add cheese and blend until smooth.

196

∾ POPPY SEED DRESSING

Makes about 1 1/2 cups

1/2 cup sugar
1 teaspoon dry mustard
1 teaspoon Hungarian paprika
2 tablespoons white wine vinegar
3 tablespoons red wine vinegar
1 cup canola oil
2 teaspoons poppy seeds

- Combine sugar, dry mustard, paprika, and vinegars in a blender container. Cover; process until smooth.
- Slowly add canola oil, while blender is still running, and process until dressing is thick.
- Add poppy seeds and stir for 1 minute.
- Pour into a glass container and refrigerate.

∾ HOUSE RANCH DRESSING

Makes about 2 1/2 cups

1 cup mayonnaise
1 cup buttermilk
2 tablespoons finely chopped green onions
2 tablespoons chopped parsley
1/4 teaspoon garlic powder
1/4 teaspoon ground cumin
2 drops hot sauce
Dash of paprika
Salt and pepper to taste

- Combine all ingredients in blender container; process until smooth. Cover and refrigerate.
- Make ahead to allow flavors to blend.

〰️ PESTO SALAD DRESSING

Makes 1 1/2 cups

1/4 cup minced parsley
1/4 cup minced fresh basil or 1 tablespoon dried basil
1 clove garlic, crushed
1/4 cup olive oil
1/4 cup chicken broth
1/4 cup red wine vinegar
4 teaspoons Dijon mustard
2 teaspoons sugar
1/2 teaspoon salt
Fresh ground pepper to taste

- In a small bowl, combine all ingredients and mix well. Cover and refrigerate for at least 1 hour.
- Serve as a dressing for tossed salad, or can also be used as a sauce over pasta.

〰️ FRENCH MUSTARD DRESSING

Makes approximately 1 cup

2 hard-cooked eggs, chopped
1 1/2 teaspoons salt
1 1/2 teaspoons sugar
1 teaspoon coarsely-ground pepper
1 tablespoon Dijon mustard
1 tablespoon chopped fresh parsley
1 large clove garlic, mashed
1/2 cup extra-virgin olive oil
5 tablespoons cream
1/4 cup white wine vinegar

- Place ingredients in blender and blend for 30 seconds to 1 minute. Dressing can also be mixed by hand with ingredients added in the order given.
- Toss lightly with a salad of leafy lettuces such as endive, escarole, chicory, green and red leaf lettuce, romaine, or Boston for best results.

BREADS

(Page 199) Robert Doisneau (French, born 1912), *Boulangerie, Rue de Poitou,* 1971. Gelatin silver print, 9 3/4 x 12 inches. Gift of John Rudolf.

As a young man, Robert Doisneau became fascinated with photography and chose to use the medium to express his deep feelings for his beloved Paris. Since 1930 he has been recording, with humor, irony, affection, and compassion, the people and neighborhoods of the City of Lights. His ouvre stands as a record of twentieth-century Paris, showing how it has changed and, more importantly, despite fashion and fad, how the city and its people remain timeless.

BREADS

Yeast Breads

Quick Breads

❧ FAIRY BUTTER

Beat the yolks of two hard eggs in a marble mortar, with some orange flower water, and two to three tea spoonfuls of fine sugar pounded [*blend together 2 hard boiled egg yolks, 1 teaspoon sugar, and if you wish, 1 teaspoon orange flower water*]; take the same weight of fresh churned butter as you have of the other ingredients [*1/4 cup*]; make it as fine as paste, and pass it through a silver strainer into a china plate. It is very pretty at a cold entertainment.

❧ PUMPERNICKEL RYE

Makes 2 26–ounce loaves

5 [1/4–ounce] packages yeast
1 3/4 cups water
1/4 cup plus 2 tablespoons molasses
1 tablespoon caraway seeds
1 tablespoon salt
2 tablespoons vegetable oil
2 cups pumpernickel flour
1 to 2 cups all-purpose flour

- Mix all ingredients, except all-purpose flour, together in a large bowl. Add all-purpose flour slowly and carefully to make extremely wet dough, using as much of the flour as necessary. With mixer speed on 2 low, beat with mixer for 5 minutes.
- Let dough rise for 1 1/2 hours.
- Divide dough in half and shape into 2 loaves; place on a flat baking sheet. Let rise until double in volume, about 1 hour.
- Bake at 400° about 30 minutes, until light brown. Test for doneness.

The first bread recipe is not for bread, but for a bread accompaniment, and comes from *The Modern Art of Cookery*. We have tried it; it is delicious, albeit a bit unusual. We were enchanted by the name, and while we feel a "silver strainer" is not absolutely necessary, Fairy Butter makes a wonderful addition to cold meat, vegetable, or tea sandwiches.

The first two yeast bread recipes come from a Birmingham bakery that has quickly gained a reputation as one of the finest places in the area for baked goods; particularly bread. Continental Bakery is located in English Village on Cahaba Road, just over the mountain. Their first recipe is for a rich, brown pumpernickel that will make your efforts well worthwhile.

201

The second bread recipe from Continental Bakery is a good alternative for people allergic to yeast. This traditional Irish bread has quite an unusual taste and texture for those who are expecting the usual bread. But it is a delicious change from the norm for all bread lovers.

❧ IRISH SODA BREAD
(Good for people who are allergic to yeast)
Makes 2 loaves

3 1/2 cups flour
Pinch of salt
1 tablespoon baking powder
1 teaspoon baking soda
3 tablespoons sugar
3 tablespoons shortening
1 egg
1 to 1 1/4 cups buttermilk

• Mix all dry ingredients together in a bowl.
• Cut in shortening.
• Add egg and buttermilk to dry mix.
• Mix by hand or with a wooden spoon, not a mixer. Dough will be sticky.
• Shape into 2 round, flat loaves.
• Bake at 375° to 400° for about 30 minutes, until golden brown.

Buttermilk can be made by mixing together 1 1/4 cups reconstituted evaporated milk, or whole milk, with 1 tablespoon white vinegar.

This bread recipe comes from Vincent's Market. As with Continental's Irish soda bread, egg bread is not your normal white bread. It is more dense with a rich, yellow color and is particularly popular in eastern Europe and the middle east. The most wonderful quality, however, for those who entertain, is that it can be molded into bread sculptures that are beautiful to look at, yet good to eat! We have listed some of the more popular shapes as recommended by Vincent's; let your imagination be your guide.

❧ BRAIDED EGG BREAD
2 [1/4–ounce] packages instant dry yeast
2 1/2 cups warm milk
2 teaspoons salt
Pinch of sugar
5 cups bread flour
1 whole egg

• Form a cavity in flour mixture. Pour remaining ingredients into the cavity.
• Mix lightly and knead dough until smooth and flexible.
• Place in a greased bowl, cover with a cloth, and let rise until double in volume, 1 to 2 hours.
• Shape into loaves (see shapes below) and let rise for 50 to 60 more minutes.
• Bake at 425° for 25 to 30 minutes, or until golden brown.

This dough can be made into the following:
Twist rolls, Baskets, Stars, Hearts, Flowers, Animals: Turtles, rabbits, alligators, etc.

༺ CHALLAH

Makes 2 loaves

2 [1/4–ounce] packages instant yeast
Approximately 5 cups unbleached flour
2 tablespoons sugar
2 teaspoons salt
1/3 cup shortening
1 cup water
3 eggs, plus 1 egg white

- Combine yeast, about 2 cups of flour, sugar, salt, and shortening.
- Add warmed water [120° to 130°] and mix on medium speed in mixer for about 2 minutes.
- Add eggs and egg white, and beat at high speed for another 2 minutes. Batter will be thick and sticky.
- With a dough hook, add additional flour, 1 cup at a time, until dough is no longer sticky and it cleans the sides of the bowl.
- Knead either by hand or using dough hook for about 10 minutes.
- Place in a greased bowl, cover, and let rise until double in volume, about 45 minutes.
- Punch down, divide evenly into 2 pieces. For the traditional braid, divide each half into 3 equal pieces, roll them into cylinders, and braid, pinching the ends together.
- Brush with an eggwash, sprinkle with poppy seeds, and let rise until double in size [about 45 minutes].
- Bake at 400° for 30 to 40 minutes, until golden brown and hollow sounding when tapped lightly on the bottom.

Our next bread recipe has also been contributed by Continental Bakery. This bread is rich in tradition, and is baked for festive occasions. Shaped like a braid, it is sprinkled with poppy seeds before baking.

203

Betty K. Grisham served a lovely and memorable luncheon at her home in Huntsville for a group of BMA museum members, and the Huntsville museum director, curators, and some of their board members. The trip and the meal were delightful, including the saffron bread. We have included her recipe and recommend taking the extra time and effort to make this delicious homemade bread.

❧ SAFFRON BREAD

Makes 14 to 16 slices per loaf

1 cup milk, scalded
1/8 to 1/4 teaspoon crushed saffron
1/2 cup butter
2 teaspoons salt
1/4 cup sugar
2 packages yeast
1/4 cup warm water
3 eggs
1 teaspoon grated lemon rind
4 1/2 cups all-purpose flour

- Crumble saffron into heating milk and scald. Remove from heat and add salt, sugar, and butter, allowing butter to melt as the mixture cools.
- Soften the yeast in 1/4 cup warm water.
- When milk is lukewarm, add yeast to the milk mixture; stir well.
- Beat three eggs with grated lemon rind and mix into milk.
- Stir in flour.
- Knead the dough 5 minutes, about 300 times.
- Set in a warm place and let dough rise till double in bulk.
- Punch down and form the dough into loaves in 2 greased loaf pans.
- Let double in bulk again.
- Bake at 375° for 25 minutes, until nicely browned.
- Remove from pans and let cool. Brush with melted butter.

❧ BROCCOLI CORNBREAD PIE

Serves 8 to 10

1 [8 1/2–ounce] box cornbread mix
4 eggs, beaten
1 [10–ounce] package frozen chopped broccoli, thawed and drained
1 onion, chopped
2 cups [8 ounces] grated Cheddar cheese
1/4 cup melted margarine

- Grease a deep-dish pie pan.
- Mix ingredients together.
- Pour into pan.
- Bake at 350° for 20 to 30 minutes, until golden.
- Cut into wedges and serve.

❧ JALAPEÑO CORNBREAD

Serves 10 to 12

2 1/2 cups cornmeal
1 cup all-purpose flour
2 tablespoons sugar
1 tablespoon salt
4 teaspoons baking powder
3 eggs
1 [16–ounce] can cream-style corn
2 cups [8 ounces] grated sharp Cheddar cheese
1 large onion, chopped
1 1/2 cups milk
1/2 cup cooking oil
1/2 cup chopped jalapeños (or to taste)

- In a bowl, combine cornmeal, flour, sugar, salt, and baking powder.
- In a separate bowl, beat eggs.
- Stir in milk and cooking oil.
- Add liquid to cornmeal mix.
- Stir in cream-style corn, cheese, onion, and jalapeño peppers.
- Pour into 2 greased 9 x 12–inch pans.
- Bake at 425° for 25 minutes.

Great with chili.

205

❧ SPOON BREAD

Serves 5 to 6

2 cups milk
1 teaspoon salt
3/4 cup white cornmeal
3 tablespoons butter
3 eggs, separated

- Heat the milk with the salt.
- Gradually add cornmeal, stirring briskly with a whisk.
- Cook slowly until mixture is very thick.
- Remove from heat, and stir in butter. Cool.
- Beat in egg yolks, after adding a little meal to yolks first to keep the eggs from over-heating.
- Beat egg whites until stiff and fold into cornmeal mixture.
- Turn into a generously buttered 2–quart soufflé dish.
- Bake at 350° for 30 minutes.
- Serve immediately.

 **RICH MAN'S BISCUITS**

Serves 8

1 cup self-rising flour
1/2 cup milk
1 rounded tablespoon mayonnaise

- Place ingredients in a small bowl and beat thoroughly with a fork.
- Drop from a spoon into a heavy shallow skillet, or divide evenly into 8 muffin tins.
- Bake at 375° for 10 to 12 minutes.

Fast and easy, crispy on the outside

POPOVERS

Makes 6

1 cup milk
1 cup all-purpose flour
2 eggs
1/2 teaspoon salt
6 cold, greased, deep 6–ounce custard cups

- Put all ingredients in a mixing bowl.
- Stir quickly with a spoon till moist, but not necessarily smooth.
- Fill cold, greased custard cups half full with mixture.
- Place the custard cups in a cold oven and set the oven for 450°; bake for 30 minutes.
- Keep oven door closed while baking.
- Serve immediately.

207

❧ PINEAPPLE BREAD

Serves 12 to 15

2 cups all-purpose flour
1 teaspoon baking powder
1/4 teaspoon salt
3/4 cup sugar
1 cup nuts
1 cup raisins
1 egg, beaten
1 teaspoon vanilla
2 tablespoons salad oil
1 [8 1/4–ounce] can crushed pineapple with juice
1 teaspoon baking soda

- Mix all ingredients together at one time, except pineapple and soda.
- Stir soda into the pineapple and add to the other mixture.
- Mix and pour into a greased and floured 8 1/2 x 4 1/2–inch loaf pan.
- Bake at 350° for about 1 hour, or until a toothpick comes out clean.

❧ WHOLE WHEAT BANANA BREAD

Makes 20 to 24 slices

1 cup honey
1 cup margarine
3 large ripe bananas
4 eggs, lightly beaten
1 1/2 cups whole wheat flour
1 1/2 cups all-purpose flour
1 tablespoon baking powder
1/2 teaspoon salt
1 teaspoon nutmeg
1/2 cup milk
1 teaspoon vanilla

- Blend honey and margarine together till creamy.
- Add mashed bananas and beat well.
- Stir in eggs.
- Combine dry ingredients and add alternately with milk to the batter.
- Stir in vanilla.
- Pour into two greased and floured 9 x 5–inch loaf pans.
- Bake at 350° for 50 minutes.
- Cool for 10 minutes before removing from pan.

❧ LEMON BREAD

Makes 1 loaf

1/2 cup shortening
1 cup sugar
2 eggs
1 1/2 cups all-purpose flour
1 1/2 teaspoons baking powder
1/4 teaspoon salt
1/2 cup milk
Grated rind of 1 lemon
1/2 cup chopped nuts (optional)
Glaze (recipe follows)

- Combine shortening and sugar, blending until light and fluffy.
- Add eggs, one at a time, beating after each addition.
- Combine flour, baking powder, and salt; add to blended mixture alternately with milk, mixing well after each addition.
- Stir in lemon rind; add nuts, if desired.
- Pour batter into a well-greased 9 x 5 x 3–inch loaf pan.
- Bake at 350° for 60 minutes.
- Pour glaze over bread. Cool 10 to 15 minutes before removing from pan.

Glaze

Makes about 1/3 cup

1/3 cup sugar
2 tablespoons lemon juice

- Combine sugar and lemon juice, mixing well.

209

OATMEAL BREAD

Serves 12 to 15

1 1/4 cups boiling water
1 cup oatmeal
1 cup sugar
1/2 cup margarine
1 cup firmly packed brown sugar
1 teaspoon vanilla
2 eggs
1 1/2 cups all-purpose flour
1 teaspoon soda
1/2 teaspoon salt
3/4 teaspoon cinnamon
1/4 teaspoon nutmeg
Frosting (recipe follows)

- Pour boiling water over oatmeal; cover and let stand for 20 minutes.
- Beat margarine till creamy.
- Gradually add sugars and beat till fluffy.
- Blend in vanilla and eggs.
- Stir in oatmeal mixture.
- Sift flour, soda, salt, cinnamon, and nutmeg together. Add to mixture.
- Pour into a well-greased and floured loaf pan.
- Bake at 350° for 50 to 55 minutes. Remove from oven, but not from pan.
- Spread frosting evenly over bread.
- Broil until frosting bubbles quickly.
- Serve warm or cold.

Frosting

1/4 cup margarine
1/2 cup packed brown sugar
3 tablespoons half-and-half
1/3 cup chopped nuts
3/4 cup flaked coconut

- Combine all ingredients.

❧ WALNUT ONION BREAD

Serves 10 to 12

3 cups all-purpose flour
1/3 cup sugar
1 tablespoon baking powder
1/2 teaspoon baking soda
1 teaspoon salt
1 cup chopped walnuts
1 1/2 cups buttermilk
4 tablespoons melted butter
1/2 cup minced onions

- Grease a round 2–quart casserole.
- Combine dry ingredients in a bowl.
- With a fork, blend in buttermilk, onions, walnuts, and butter until all are evenly mixed.
- Turn onto a lightly floured surface and knead 2 to 3 minutes, forming a ball. Dough will be slightly sticky.
- Place in casserole, score the top with an "X".
- Bake for 1 hour and 15 minutes at 350°, until a toothpick comes clean.
- Remove from dish and cool on a wire rack.

Serve with soft cheeses such as Brie or Camembert.

❧ APRICOT COFFEE CAKE

Serves 10 to 12

2 cups all-purpose flour
2 teaspoons baking powder
1/2 teaspoon soda
1/2 teaspoon salt
1 cup brown sugar
4 tablespoons butter
2 eggs, beaten
1 cup sour cream
1 teaspoon vanilla
3/4 cup stewed and drained apricots, fresh or dried
Streusel topping (recipe follows)

- Sift all dry ingredients together.
- Cut in butter.
- Combine eggs, sour cream, and vanilla. Stir into dry ingredients.
- Pour into a deep 12–inch pie plate.
- Place stewed apricots over top of batter.
- Sprinkle with streusel topping.
- Bake 40 minutes at 350°.

Streusel topping

1/2 cup brown sugar
2 tablespoons all-purpose flour
1 teaspoon grated lemon rind
2 tablespoons melted butter
1/2 cup chopped nuts

- Mix all streusel ingredients together till crumbly.

David Teniers the Younger, (Flemish, 1610–90), *Tavern Scene*, mid-seventeenth century. Oil on canvas. 21 x 30 inches. Gift of Frank Lankford.

David Teniers the Younger, renowned among Flemish genre painters, was the most famous member of an artistic family. He achieved great success during his lifetime, becoming court painter to Archduke Leopold Wilhelm, regent of Netherlands, and was curator of the archduke's collection, one of the finest at that time. He was also an intimate friend of Rubens and son-in-law of Jan Brugehel the Elder.

Tavern Scene is a wonderful example of seventeenth-century genre paintings which concentrated on serene interior tableaux, such as *Kitchen Interior* (page 169), or on common peasant scenes as shown in this Teniers' painting. These paintings were didactic, and attempted to teach the viewer of the brevity of life and the benefits in living it wisely. Dedication to hard work and perseverance with common chores were honorable and noble acts that earned one rewards in the next life, while drink and debauchery would not earn peace of mind in this life nor heaven in the next.

∾ BLUEBERRY COFFEE CAKE

Serves 8 to 10

3 cups all-purpose flour
1 1/2 teaspoons baking powder
3/4 teaspoon baking soda
1/2 teaspoon salt
1/4 cup brown sugar
1 tablespoon all-purpose flour
1/2 teaspoon cinnamon
3/4 cup margarine
1 1/2 cups sugar
1 teaspoon vanilla
4 eggs
1 cup sour cream
2 cups fresh blueberries
1 cup powdered sugar
1 to 2 tablespoons milk

- Sift flour, baking powder, soda, and salt.
- Combine brown sugar with 1 tablespoon of flour and cinnamon.
- Beat butter, sugar, and vanilla till fluffy.
- Add eggs, one at a time, beating after each addition.
- Beat in flour mix alternately with sour cream.
- Turn 1/3 of batter into a greased tube pan.
- Sprinkle with 1/2 of blueberries and 1/2 brown sugar. Repeat layering.
- Top with last 1/3 of batter.
- Bake at 350° for 1 hour.
- Cool, and remove gently from pan.
- Mix powdered sugar and milk till smooth and drizzle over cake.

214

～ SOUR CREAM COFFEE CAKE

Serves 6 to 8

1/2 cup margarine
1 cup sugar
2 eggs
2 cups all-purpose flour
1 teaspoon salt
1 teaspoon baking powder
1 teaspoon baking soda
1 [8–ounce] carton sour cream
1 teaspoon vanilla

Topping

1/2 cup sugar
2 teaspoons cinnamon

- Mix sugar and cinnamon together; set aside.
- Blend margarine and sugar together.
- Add eggs, one at a time.
- Add dry ingredients alternately with sour cream and vanilla.
- Put half the batter in a round 8 or 9–inch cake pan.
- Add half the topping and repeat layers.
- Swirl the mixture with a knife to lightly blend the topping and batter.
- Bake at 350° for 40 minutes.

∽ CHIVE-PARMESAN SCONES

Makes 10

1 1/2 cups all-purpose flour
1 cup grated Parmesan cheese
1 tablespoon baking powder
1/4 teaspoon salt
1/4 teaspoon pepper
1/4 cup margarine
2 tablespoons olive oil
2 tablespoons honey
1 egg, beaten
1/2 cup heavy cream
3 tablespoons chopped chives
2 cloves garlic, crushed
Ground cayenne pepper

- Combine dry ingredients, and cut in margarine until the mixture resembles coarse meal.
- Stir in remaining ingredients, except cayenne pepper, until the dough holds together.
- Drop by large spoonfuls onto a greased baking sheet, about an inch apart.
- Sprinkle lightly with cayenne pepper.
- Bake for 8 to 10 minutes at 400°.

❧ SOUR CREAM BRAN MUFFINS

Makes 8 muffins

1/2 cup butter or margarine, softened
1/4 cup firmly packed brown sugar
1 egg
1 cup sour cream
1/4 cup molasses
1 1/2 cups raisins
1 cup all-purpose flour
1 teaspoon baking soda
1/4 teaspoon salt
1 cup wheat bran cereal

- Cream butter. Gradually add sugar, beating well.
- Add egg, sour cream, and molasses. Mix well and add raisins.
- Combine flour, soda, salt, and cereal. Stir into mixture.
- Fill muffin tin and bake at 300° for 30 minutes.

This is the second of two bread recipes from Vincent's; this one is for healthy and delicious muffins. Muffins have enjoyed a resurgence in popularity recently, and with easy, tasty recipes like this, we can understand why.

❧ POPPY SEED MUFFINS

Makes 9 to 12

1 1/2 cups biscuit mix
3/4 cup sour cream
1/4 cup sugar
1 egg
1 teaspoon vanilla
2 tablespoons poppy seeds
3/4 cup raisins

- Mix biscuit mix, sour cream, sugar, egg, and vanilla together by hand until they are well blended.
- Add poppy seeds and raisins; stir.
- Fill greased muffin tins 2/3 full.
- Bake at 400° for 17 minutes or until light golden in color.

These easy-to-make muffins are a favorite of the musem's membership coordinator, Kristin Manthey. The unusual taste combination of the poppy seeds, sour cream, and raisins is a delightful surprise.

217

❧ LEMON MUFFINS

Makes 18 muffins or 12 giant muffins

2 cups self-rising flour
1 [3 1/4–ounce] box lemon instant pudding
2 tablespoons sugar
1/4 cup oil
1 1/3 cups milk
Powdered sugar

- Mix flour, pudding, and sugar.
- Add liquid all at once; stir only till moistened.
- Fill greased muffin tins 2/3 full.
- Bake at 425° for 20 to 25 minutes.
- Sprinkle with powdered sugar.

This recipe is from the museum's former membership coordinator, Leah Boston Hathcock. It is quick, easy, and delicious, the perfect recipe for a busy career-oriented person who still wants to have quality time at home with friends and family.

218

❧ BLUEBERRY LEMON MUFFINS

Makes 12

1 3/4 cups all-purpose flour
1/4 cup sugar
2 1/2 teaspoons baking powder
3/4 teaspoon salt
3/4 cup milk
1 egg, beaten
1/3 cup vegetable oil
1 cup fresh blueberries
2 tablespoons sugar
1/4 teaspoon grated lemon rind
1/4 cup melted butter
1/4 cup sugar

- Sift flour, sugar, baking powder, and salt together.
- Combine milk, egg, and oil; add all at once to dry ingredients.
- Stir quickly just till moistened.
- Toss blueberries with sugar and lemon rind.
- Stir into batter gently.
- Fill greased muffin tins 2/3 full.
- Bake at 400° for 25 minutes.
- While warm, dip the tops in the melted butter, then in the sugar.

POLLY'S DILL MUFFINS

Makes 24 mini muffins

1 cup self-rising flour
1/2 cup margarine
1/2 cup sour cream
2 teaspoons dill seed

- Cut margarine into flour; when mixture is crumbly, add sour cream and dill seed and blend.
- Put rounded teaspoonfuls of mixture in mini-muffin tins.
- Bake at 400° for 15 to 20 minutes.
- Slice and serve plain or with thinly sliced ham.

 CHEESE AND PEPPER MUFFINS

Makes 1 1/2 dozen

2 1/2 cups all-purpose
1/4 cup yellow cornmeal
1/4 cup sugar
2 tablespoons baking powder
1/2 teaspoon salt
1/4 teaspoon red pepper
3/4 cup [3 ounces] shredded sharp Cheddar cheese
1/4 cup finely chopped onion
3 tablespoons finely chopped green pepper
1 [2–ounce] jar diced pimento, drained
2 eggs, beaten
1 1/2 cups milk
1/4 cup vegetable oil

- Combine first 10 ingredients in a large bowl; make a well in center of mixture.
- Combine eggs, milk, and oil; add to dry ingredients, stirring just until moistened.
- Spoon into greased muffin pans, filling 2/3 full.
- Bake at 400° for 20 to 25 minutes.
- Remove from pans immediately.

❧ BANANA FRITTERS

Makes 6 to 8

1 1/4 cups all-purpose flour
1 1/2 teaspoons baking powder
2 heaping tablespoons sugar
1/4 teaspoon salt
1/2 cup milk
2 eggs, beaten
4 ripe bananas, sliced
Hot oil for cooking
Powdered sugar

- Sift the flour, baking powder, sugar, and salt together. Add the milk and beaten eggs. Mix well.
- Fold in the sliced bananas and drop by tablespoonfuls into the hot oil at 450° on a candy thermometer. Fry until golden in color, turning once. Remove from oil and drain on paper towels.
- Sprinkle with powdered sugar and serve.

DESSERTS

(Page 221) John Singer Sargent (American, 1856–1925), *Portrait of Lady Helen Vincent, Viscountess D'Abernon*, 1904. Oil on canvas, 62 1/2 x 42 1/2 inches. Museum purchase with funds from John Bohorfoush, the 1984 Beaux Arts Committee, and the Museum Store.

John Singer Sargent was one of the premire portrait painters of the late nineteenth and early twentieth centuries. He earned his reputation on both sides of the Atlantic by doing large, full figure canvases, rich in color and with a loose brushstroke that revealed the sensuous textures of the fabrics in his paintings. This commission portrays one of the most beautiful and elegant ladies in early twentieth century England. Painted in Venice, the portrait exemplifies these characteristics, but also focuses on her strength and intelligence. She worked as a trained anesthetist during World War I, and was a member of the exclusive intellectual circle known as The Souls, which was comprised of the most influential and creative figures of the day.

DESSERTS

❧ BENEDIKT'S RED VELVET CAKE

Serves 16 to 20

1/2 cup shortening
1 1/2 cups sugar
2 eggs
2 tablespoons cocoa
2 tablespoons margarine, melted
2 tablespoons red food coloring
1 tablespoon vanilla extract
2 cups all-purpose flour
1 teaspoon salt
1 cup plus 2 tablespoons buttermilk
1 1/4 teaspoons baking soda
2 tablespoons cider vinegar
Cream cheese icing (recipe follows)

- Beat shortening and sugar together until creamy.
- Add eggs, one at a time, beating until fluffy.
- Beat in cocoa and margarine until mixture is smooth.
- Add red food coloring and vanilla; mix.
- Sift flour and salt together.
- Add flour and buttermilk alternately to batter.
- Mix baking soda and vinegar in a tall glass; add to batter, mixing on low speed.
- Divide batter into 2 greased and floured 9–inch round cake pans.
- Bake at 360° for 30 to 35 minutes.
- Remove cake from pans and cool on wire racks, then chill cakes in freezer before frosting.
- Spread icing on cake layers that have cooled in the freezer.

Cream Cheese Icing

16 ounces cream cheese
1/2 cup margarine
1 [1–pound] box powdered sugar, sifted
1 tablespoon vanilla

- Beat cream cheese and margarine together until smooth; add sugar slowly while beating, then add vanilla. Frost cake.
- Keep cake refrigerated after frosting.

Red Velvet Cake is a long-time favorite of Southern cooks. This recipe comes from Ruth and Joice Benedikt who prepared it for the museum Volunteers at Benedikt's restaurant. The restaurant sits at the top of Straight Mountain, near Springville, Alabama. Benedikt's is noted for real downhome Southern cooking, and their Red Velvet Cake is an outstanding example.

223

❧ BITTERSWEET CHOCOLATE TERRINE

Serves 16 to 20

2/3 cup shelled pistachio nuts, divided
1/2 cup golden raisins
1/2 cup halved red cherries
1 [16-ounce package] vanilla sandwich cookies with chocolate filling, crumbled
6 ounces bittersweet chocolate
2/3 cup sugar
4 tablespoons water
1 cup cocoa
3/4 cup butter, softened
1 tablespoon Grand Marnier
1 egg plus 2 yolks
2 to 3 tablespoons cocoa

- Oil a 5 x 8–inch terrine.
- Peel the pistachios by placing them briefly in boiling water. Let them set 5 minutes, drain, wrap in a towel and rub lightly to peel.
- Combine 1/3 cup of the nuts with the raisins, cherries, and crumbled cookies.
- Stir sugar and water in sauce pan over low heat until syrup is clear. Add chocolate and stir until chocolate is melted.
- Beat cocoa and butter in a bowl until smooth; add sugar syrup, melted chocolate, and Grand Marnier.
- Beat eggs; add to the above mixture.
- Gently fold in the fruit/cookie mix and press into terrine and tap firmly on counter to settle.
- Cover and refrigerate overnight. To unmold, place in warm water, run a knife around edges, and turn out of terrine.
- Sift the 2 to 3 tablespoons of cocoa on top of the uncut terrine.
- Chop the remaining 1/3 cup of nuts and border top of terrine.
- Slice and serve in overlapping slices to show mosaic of nuts and fruits.

❧ HUNGARIAN CHOCOLATE CAKE

Serves 8 to 10

10 egg yolks
2/3 cup sugar
10 tablespoons butter
8 ounces bittersweet or German sweet chocolate
1 cup very finely ground pecans
   (This is best done in a fine grater or nut grinder and the texture
   should be as fine and fluffy as flour)
8 egg whites
3/4 cup apricot preserves
2/3 cup chopped pecans

- In a large bowl, mix yolks and sugar together, stirring gently occasionally to dissolve the sugar.
- Place butter and chocolate in the top of a double boiler and heat gently until mixture is smooth.
- Slowly stir melted chocolate mixture into egg yolk and sugar mixture until blended.
- Remove 1 cup and set aside to use as frosting for cake. Fold the ground pecans into mixture remaining in the bowl.
- Beat egg whites until stiff but not dry.
- Stir 1/4 of the egg whites into nut mixture. Gently fold in remaining whites.
- Pour mixture into a greased and floured 8–inch springform pan and bake at 350° for 50 to 60 minutes or until center feels springy to the touch.
- Set pan on a rack to cool and gently ease a spatula around the edge so cake falls evenly as it cools. When cool, remove from pan. Transfer cake to a serving dish. Slice into 2 layers and spread preserves over bottom layer. Replace top layer.
- If frosting mixture is not stiff enough to spread, refrigerate for 20 to 30 minutes. Frost top and sides of cake, and sprinkle nuts on top. Refrigerate until served.
- The cake can be made a day ahead, but should be stored in the refrigerator.

225

❧ CHOCOLATE AMARETTI TORTE

Serves 8 to 10

1 cup butter
1 cup sugar
5 eggs, separated
1/2 cup all-purpose flour
1/2 cup amaretto-flavored macaroons, crushed (Amaretti di Soronno are best)
4 squares semi-sweet chocolate
Powdered sugar

- Beat butter and sugar together until creamy.
- Beat in egg yolks one at a time, and beat for 10 minutes.
- Gradually add flour and Amaretti crumbs.
- Fold in finely grated chocolate.
- Beat egg whites until they are stiff, and fold into mixture.
- Pour into a 10–inch well-greased round pan.
- Bake for 35 to 45 minutes at 350°.
- Sprinkle with powdered sugar and serve.

Whipped cream and fresh berries are nice with this.

～ CHOCOLATE ROULAGE

Serves 8 to 12

6 tablespoons cake flour
6 tablespoons unsweet cocoa
1/2 teaspoon baking powder
1/4 teaspoon salt
4 egg whites
3/4 cup sugar
4 egg yolks
1 teaspoon vanilla
2 tablespoons confectioner's sugar mixed with 2 tablespoons cocoa

Filling
1 pint [2 cups] whipping cream
1/2 cup confectioner's sugar
2 teaspoons vanilla

- Line a 9 x 14 x 1–inch jelly roll pan with greased wax paper.
- Sift cake flour, cocoa, baking powder, and salt together 3 times.
- Beat egg whites until stiff, but not dry. Gradually beat in sugar.
- Beat egg yolks until thick and lemon colored; add vanilla and mix.
- Fold yolk mixture into the whites, then gently fold in the flour mixture.
- Gently pour the batter into the lined pan and spread evenly.
- Bake for 12 minutes at 400°.
- Remove from oven, immediately turn onto a towel dusted with the confectioner's sugar and cocoa, and gently remove wax paper from sponge cake. While still hot, roll the cake and towel and let set until cool.
- Make filling by whipping the cream, confectioner's sugar, and vanilla together until stiff peaks form.
- Unroll the cool cake, and spread filling on inside; roll up, place on a serving plate, and dust with more confectioner's sugar and cocoa.

⌒ MAHOGANY POUND CAKE

Serves 12 to 15

2 1/2 cups all-purpose flour
1/2 cup cocoa
1 cup butter, softened
2 cups sugar
1 cup brown sugar
6 eggs, separated
1 cup sour cream
1 teaspoon vanilla
1/4 teaspoon baking soda

- Sift flour and cocoa together; set aside.
- In a large bowl, combine butter and sugars; beat until light and fluffy.
- Add 6 egg yolks, one at a time, beating well after each addition.
- Stir in vanilla.
- Combine sour cream and baking soda; add to creamed mixture alternately with dry ingredients.
- Beat 6 egg whites until stiff; fold into batter.
- Pour into a well-greased and floured 10–inch tube pan.
- Bake 1 1/2 hours at 325°, until toothpick comes out clean.

⌒ TO MAKE A POUND CAKE

Set a pound of flour before the fire to dry, and then let it stand to be cold; beat a pound of butter in an earthenware pan one way, till it is like a thick cream, beat up twelve eggs, (leaving out six whites) strain them into the butter, with a pound of sugar sifted, and a few carraways; stir these well together, then dust in the flour, and with a pudding stirrer, beat it very well for an hour; butter a pan, and bake it an hour in a quick oven.

For a change you may add currants instead of carraways.

228

This Pound Cake recipe, from *The Modern Art of Cookery,* is more for your enjoyment than anything else. It is the traditional pound-of-everything recipe, and makes a very large cake. We have not updated the instructions; they are fairly easy to understand and follow. We will assume anyone brave enough to use this recipe will know you do not have to dry the flour before the fire, and will have second and third thoughts about proceeding when they get to the instructions about beating it for an hour.

ᕬᔆ SOUR CREAM APPLE PIE

Serves 6 to 8

9–inch pastry shell, uncooked
2 cups thinly sliced apples
3/4 cup sugar
1/2 teaspoon vanilla
1 egg, beaten
1/3 teaspoon salt
1 cup sour cream
2 teaspoons flour

Topping

1/4 cup melted butter
1/3 cup plus 2 tablespoons flour
3/4 cup brown sugar
• Mix ingredients together with a fork.

• Mix sugar, vanilla, egg, salt, sour cream, and flour together.
• Add sliced apples and mix well.
• Pour into an unbaked pie shell.
• Bake at 350° for 45 minutes.
• Cover with topping and return to oven for another 20 minutes.

Serve hot topped with ice cream or whipped cream.

We open the section on pies with two recipes for apple pies, one new, one old, and both delicious. Our first apple pie comes from the Back Alley restaurant where it is one of the dessert favorites. It is a fairly simple recipe that is delicious when served hot with cold whipped cream or ice cream.

229

ᕬᔆ A NICE APPLE PYE

Take codlings, or the clearest apples you can get [*6 to 8 cooking apples such as Rome, Winesap, or Jonathan*]; pare, core, and cut them in thin slices; lay a piece of puff paste round the inside of the dish [*p. 78, 2–crust pastry*]; pour in some currant jelly [*1/4 cup*], then apples, then currant jelly [*1/4 cup*]; strew in a little candied lemon-peel cut small [*1 tablespoon*], and fill your dish with apples, as full as you would have it; put in the rest of the sugar [*1/2 to 3/4 cup sugar*], lid it with a good puff paste, and it is little inferior to a sweet-meat pye. [*Seal the edges of the crust and cut the top to let the steam escape. Bake at 375° for 40 minutes or until crust is nicely browned.*]

The second apple pie recipe comes from *The Modern Art of Cookery*. It is also a fairly simple recipe, made even simpler by using a pre-made, purchased double crust, if you wish. So we have only updated the measurements. Oh, and baking instructions.
For those who prefer homemade pastry, the puff pastry recipe noted is also from *The Modern Art of Cookery*.

MARY JOHN'S FRESH BLUEBERRY PIE

Serves 6 to 8

1 quart fresh blueberries
1 cup water
1 cup sugar
2 tablespoons cornstarch
2 tablespoons water
1 cup whipping cream
1 9–inch baked pastry shell

- Wash berries; refrigerate all but 1 cup.
- Cook 1 cup of berries, water, and sugar together for 10 minutes.
- Strain cooked berry mixture.
- Add cornstarch, which has been dissolved in 2 tablespoons of water, to the strained liquid.
- Let mixture return to a boil and cook until it is thick (about 1 minute).
- Chill thoroughly.
- Put cold, uncooked berries in the pastry shell and pour cooked syrup over them.
- Top with whipped cream and serve.

ALASKAN GRAPEFRUIT PIE

Serves 8 to 10

1 9–inch baked pastry shell
1/2 cup grapefruit juice, divided
32 large marshmallows, halved
2 1/2 cups grapefruit sections
1 cup heavy cream, whipped
1/4 cup toasted coconut

- In a saucepan, melt marshmallows in 1/4 cup grapefruit juice, stirring until marshmallows are completely melted.
- Cool and stir in remaining juice.
- Fold together marshmallow mixture, grapefruit sections, and stiffly whipped cream.
- Pour mixture into the baked pastry shell.
- Refrigerate at least 3 hours.
- Sprinkle coconut over pie.
- Serve with a pony of grapefruit schnapps.

❧ PINEAPPLE CHEESE PIE

Serves 12 to 14

1 [20–ounce] can crushed pineapple, drained
1 cup sugar
3 teaspoons all-purpose flour
2 [8–ounce] packages cream cheese
1/2 cup butter or margarine
2 cups sugar
3 eggs
2 unbaked, 9–inch, deep-dish pastry shells
1/2 cup sliced almonds

- Combine the first 3 ingredients in a saucepan and cook until thick; set aside to cool.
- Beat cream cheese, butter or margarine, and sugar together.
- Add eggs and whip until fluffy.
- Divide pineapple filling evenly into 2 pastry shells.
- Pour cream cheese mixture on top of each.
- Sprinkle 1/4 cup sliced almonds on top of each pie.
- Bake at 325° for 40 to 50 minutes.

 **PUMPKIN ICE CREAM PIE**

Serves 6 to 8

1 cup pumpkin filling
1/2 cup brown sugar
1/4 teaspoon cinnamon
1/8 teaspoon nutmeg
1 quart of vanilla ice cream, softened
1 [9–inch] graham cracker crust (recipe follows)
Mincemeat Sauce (recipe follows)

- Combine pumpkin, sugar, cinnamon, and nutmeg; blend well.
- Slowly stir in the softened ice cream until it is well blended.
- Spoon into pie shell.
- Place in the freezer 3 to 4 hours or overnight.
- Serve with hot mincemeat sauce.

Graham Cracker Crust

1 1/2 cups graham cracker crumbs
1/4 cup sugar
1/4 cup finely chopped almonds
1/4 cup melted butter
1/4 teaspoon salt

- Combine all ingredients and press evenly onto the bottom and sides of a lightly greased pie plate.

Mincemeat Sauce

2 cups prepared mincemeat
1 tablespoon grated orange rind
1/2 cup apricot nectar

- Mix ingredients together and heat over low heat for 5 minutes.

❧ MACAROON PIE

Serves 6 to 8

12 saltine crackers, crushed
12 dates, finely chopped
1/2 cup chopped pecans
1 cup sugar
1/4 teaspoon baking powder
3 egg whites
1 teaspoon almond extract

- Mix first 5 ingredients together.
- Beat egg whites until they are stiff but not dry. Add almond extract.
- Fold egg whites into dry mixture.
- Pour into a well-buttered 9–inch pie plate.
- Bake for 30 minutes at 350°.
- Serve with whipped cream.

❧ CHOCOLATE CHESS PIE

Serves 6 to 8

1 stick butter or margarine
1 [1/2 ounce] chocolate
3/4 cup brown sugar
3/4 cup white sugar
1/8 teaspoon salt
2 tablespoons flour
3 tablespoons milk
2 eggs
1/2 teaspoon vanilla
1 unbaked 9–inch pastry shell

- Melt butter or margarine and chocolate together. Cool.
- Mix sugars and flour together.
- Beat eggs until yolks are mixed with whites; add dry ingredients, milk, cooled chocolate mixture, and vanilla.
- Place in an unbaked pastry shell and bake at 350° for 30 to 35 minutes.

While on an east coast vacation many years ago, Margaret and Jim Livingston enjoyed this pie at a French restaurant. To their surprise, the chef graciously shared the recipe with them, and Margaret has been serving it on special occasions ever since.

233

❧ BLACK RUSSIAN PIE

Serves 6 to 8

14 cream-filled chocolate sandwich cookies, crushed (1 cup)
2 tablespoons butter
24 marshmallows
1/2 cup milk
1/8 teaspoon salt
1/3 cup Kahlua
1 cup whipping cream
Semi-sweet chocolate curls

- Combine cookie crumbs with melted butter in an 8–inch pie plate, and press them into the pie plate to make a crust.
- Freeze until firm.
- Melt marshmallows with milk until mixture will mound on a spoon.
- Stir in Kahlua.
- Whip cream until stiff and fold into marshmallow mixture; chill for 30 minutes.
- Turn into crumb crust; freeze.
- Decorate top with curls of semi-sweet chocolate.

❧ HEAVENLY PEANUT BUTTER PIE

Serves 8 to 10

1 cup creamy peanut butter
1 [8–ounce] package cream cheese
1 cup sugar
1 teaspoon vanilla
3/4 cup whipping cream
1 9–inch chocolate-flavored crumb or graham cracker crust
2 [1–ounce] semi-sweet chocolate squares
2 tablespoons hot coffee

- Beat peanut butter, cream cheese, sugar and vanilla together until creamy.
- Beat whipping cream until soft peaks form.
- Fold whipped cream into peanut butter mixture; spoon into crust.
- Place in freezer until firm.
- Melt chocolate with coffee, stir until smooth.
- Pour chocolate over the top, spreading evenly.
- Store in the freezer.

234

PEANUT BUTTER MERINGUE PIE

Serves 8

1/3 cup peanut butter
3/4 cup sifted powdered sugar
1 9–inch baked pastry shell
1/3 cup all-purpose flour
1/2 cup sugar
1/8 teaspoon salt
2 cups scalded milk
3 egg yolks, beaten
2 tablespoons butter
1/2 teaspoon vanilla
Meringue (recipe follows)

• Blend the peanut butter and powdered sugar until mixture is mealy.
• Put 2/3 in pastry shell, reserving 1/3 as topping for the meringue.
• Combine flour, granulated sugar, and salt in top of a double boiler.
• Stir in scalded milk.
• Cook over boiling water until thick.
• Gradually stir in egg yolks.
• Cook a few minutes. Add butter and vanilla and stir.
• Pour into pie.

Meringue

3 egg whites
1/2 teaspoon vanilla
1/4 teaspoon cream of tartar
6 tablespoons sugar

• Beat egg whites with vanilla and cream of tartar until soft peaks form.
• Gradually add sugar, beating until whites are stiff and glossy.
• Immediately spread over top of the pie.
• Seal meringue at the edges of pastry.
• Sprinkle remaining peanut butter/sugar mixture on top.
• Bake at 325° for 20 minutes, until golden brown.

❧ SPECTACULAR ICE CREAM PIE

Serves 8 to 10

1 egg white
1/4 teaspoon salt
1/4 cup sugar
1 1/2 cups chopped pecans
1 pint slightly softened coffee ice cream
1 pint slightly softened vanilla ice cream
Caramel sauce (recipe follows)

- Butter a 9–inch pie pan.
- Beat egg white until stiff.
- Add salt and sugar, and fold in nuts.
- Spread in pie pan.
- Bake at 400° for 10 to 12 minutes.
- Chill.
- Add the softened ice cream in two layers.
- Cut into 8 to 10 serving pieces, cover, and freeze.
- Serve with hot caramel sauce.

Caramel Sauce

Makes 1 1/2 cups

3 tablespoons butter
1 cup light brown sugar
1/2 cup whipping cream
1 teaspoon vanilla

- Melt butter; add sugar and cook for 10 minutes, stirring constantly.
- Remove from heat and add cream, slowly, until it is blended. Heat 1 more minute.
- Add vanilla, and serve warm over pie.

❧ TO MAKE FINE APPLE DUMPLINS

Make puff paste, pare the apples and take the cores out with a scoop, then roll every apple in a piece of paste, tye them in a cloth separately and boil them an hour and a half; pare a lemon very thin, and shred the peel as fine as you can possibly, boil a tea spoon-full of it in three spoonfuls of rose, or orange flower water; take up the dumplins, and with a pen knife cut a round piece out of the crust, pour in a little melted butter, a tea spoonful of the orange flower, or lemon liquor, and some fine sugar; mix it with the apple, then lay on the piece of crust; when you have done enough for the dish, send them to table.

Puff pastry [*recipe p. 78, 1–crust pastry*]
6 cooking apples [such as Granny Smith, Rome, Jonathan]
Grated peel of 1 lemon
Juice of 1 lemon
1/4 cup melted butter
6 tablespoons brown sugar
1 teaspoon cinnamon
2 to 3 tablespoons granulated sugar

- Make puff pastry and roll into 6 8–inch circles.
- Peel and core apples and wrap each in pastry, leaving the top open.
- Mix remaining ingredients, except granulated sugar, and stuff into cavity of each apple. Twist tops closed.
- Bake at 375° for 20 minutes, sprinkle tops with granulated sugar, and bake 5 to 10 more minutes, or until crust is golden. Serve hot.

We have included a second apple recipe from *The Modern Art of Cookery*, another traditional favorite, apple dumplings. We used a separate set of instructions for baking rather than boiling, baking being more to twentieth-century tastes. If you wish to try boiling the dumplings, the original instructions work fine. These should be served hot with whipped cream.

237

 **APPLE CRUNCHIE**

Serves 4

4 large apples (cooking are best, such as Granny Smith, Rome, Jonathan)
1/2 cup sugar
1 teaspoon cinnamon
5 tablespoons water
2 to 3 tablespoons butter
3/4 cup brown sugar
3/4 cup all-purpose flour
1/4 cup butter

- Generously butter an 8 x 8–inch ovenproof dish.
- Layer sliced apples with the sugar and cinnamon and sprinkle with water.
- Cut brown sugar and flour into butter until mixture is crumbly.
- Pour over apples.
- Bake at 300° for 1 hour.

 **MRS. JARRETT'S PEACH COBBLER**

Serves 4

2 cups all-purpose flour
1 teaspoon salt
1/2 cup vegetable oil
1/4 cup milk
2 cups fresh peaches, peeled and sliced (about 4 large)
1/2 cup butter
1 cup sugar

- Mix flour and salt together.
- Pour oil and milk into flour.
- Stir with a fork until well mixed.
- Press firmly into a ball.
- Place between two sheets of waxpaper and roll thin.
- Fit the pastry into the bottom and up the sides of 1 1/2–quart round dish, with excess hanging over the sides.
- Place peaches in a saucepan to heat with the butter and sugar.
- Heat until butter melts.
- Pour into pastry, and fold pastry over the top.
- Bake for 1 hour and 10 minutes at 350°.

PINEAPPLE ANGEL DESSERT

Serves 8

2 envelopes unflavored gelatin
4 tablespoons cold water
1 cup boiling water
1 [8–ounce] can crushed pineapple, undrained
Juice of 1 lemon
1 cup sugar
2 cups whipping cream
1 prepared angel food cake, cubed
Coconut

• Soak gelatin in cold water, then dissolve in boiling water.
• Add pineapple with juice, lemon juice, and sugar.
• Refrigerate until it begins to set.
• Whip cream and fold into the mixture.
• Pour over cubed angel food cake in a flat 2–quart casserole.
• Sprinkle with coconut. Cover.
• Refrigerate overnight.

STRAWBERRIES IN BASIL SYRUP

Serves 4

1/2 cup sugar
1/2 cup water
2 tablespoons chopped fresh basil
1 quart fresh strawberries

• Combine sugar and water in a saucepan. Simmer over medium heat until sugar dissolves.
• Add chopped basil and boil until mixture is reduced to 1/2 cup. Cool. When cool, strain syrup.
• Clean and slice berries.
• Coat berries with syrup.
• Serve chilled.

An unusual, delicious dessert

This recipe from *The Modern Art of Cookery* can be found in cookbooks today in almost the exact same form. The main difference, thanks to modern technology, is that we no longer have to boil the cream. The berries can also be puréed in a blender or food processor rather than by using a sieve, and cooking them a bit longer makes a thicker mixture. Be sure to chill the berries thoroughly, and beat and stir in the cream just before you are ready to serve the fool.

 TO MAKE A STRAWBERRY AND RASBERRY FOOL

Bruise a pint of scarlet strawberries, and a pint of rasberries, pass them through a sive, and sweeten them with half a pound of fine sugar pounded [*1 cup granulated*], add a spoonful of orange flower water, then boil it over a fire, for two or three minutes [*boil, stirring, 10 to 15 minutes for a thicker berry mixture*]; take it off, and set on a pint and a half of [*heavy*] cream, boil it and stir it till it is cold [*not necessary to boil the cream; keep refigerated*]; when the pulp is cold, put them together, and stir them till they are well mixed [*whip cream into soft peaks and blend with chilled berries just until mixed, it should look marbleized*]; put the fool into glasses, or basons, as you think proper.

 HUNGARIAN FROZEN BERRY CREAM IN MERINGUE

Serves 12

1 lemon
3 egg whites, room temperature
1/4 teaspoon cream of tartar
1 teaspoon vanilla
1 cup superfine sugar
1 1/2 cups puréed berries, strained to remove seeds
    strawberries, raspberries, or blueberries
1 cup plain yogurt
1 cup cottage cheese or [8 ounces] cream cheese
1/2 cup sugar
12 or more whole berries for garnish

- Cut lemon in half and squeeze out juice; set aside.
- Cut lemon shell in half and using the inside, run it over the inside of a large mixing bowl, stainless steel or copper is best, to clean bowl completely.
- Place egg whites in bowl; add cream of tartar and vanilla.
- Beat egg whites to soft peak. Gradually, a spoonful at a time, beat in the sugar until very stiff peaks form and sugar is dissolved so no graininess remains.

- Make layers as follows:
  - Place parchment or waxed paper, wax side down, on a large baking sheet.
  - Using a 9–inch round pan as a guide, draw 2 9–inch circles.
  - Spoon meringue into a pastry tube.
  - Using a number 6 tip, start at the center of the circle and pipe a spiral to the edge of the circle for the bottom layer of meringue.
  - Switch to a number 6 star tip, and repeat spiral for the top layer on the other 9–inch circle.

OR
  - Divide meringue evenly and place in the center of the circles then spread to edges so meringue is even and smooth.

- Bake meringue circles at 250° for one hour; turn oven off and without opening oven door, leave circles in oven for one more hour.
- Remove from oven, remove parchment or waxed paper, and cool on wire racks.
- Meanwhile purée cottage cheese until smooth or soften cream cheese.
- Make berry filling by creaming together sugar and cheese; stir in yogurt and lemon juice until well blended. Stir in puréed berries; mix until well blended.
- Place in freezer until almost frozen.
- When meringues are cool and berry mixture is almost frozen, assemble dessert as follows:
  - Beat berry mixture lightly so it is workable.
  - Spread mixture over bottom meringue, almost to the edges.
  - Top with second meringue and garnish with whole or halved berries.
- Chill till stiff, then cut into slices and serve.

Keep in freezer if not serving immediately.

241

❧ BOURBON PEACHES

Serves 6 to 8

8 to 10 fresh peaches, peeled and sliced
1/4 cup bourbon
1/4 cup brown sugar

- Mix all ingredients gently; cover and refrigerate.
- Serve with crisp cookies.

Best when served over orange sherbet, vanilla ice cream, or frozen yogurt.

❧ BRANDY COMPOTE

Serves 18

2 [16–ounce] cans pear halves
2 [16–ounce] cans peach halves
1 [16–ounce] can apricots
1 [16–ounce] can pitted Bing cherries
1/2 cup brown sugar
12 coconut macaroons, crumbled
1 cup brandy, any flavor

- Drain fruit thoroughly.
- Combine macaroons and sugar.
- In a shallow 9 x 13—inch baking dish, alternate layers of the fruit and macaroon crumbs, reserving some crumbs for the top.
- Pour 3/4 cup brandy over the fruit at least 2 hours before baking.
- Add remaining brandy and bake at 350° for 1 hour. Serve hot.

Georgia O'Keeffe (American, 1887–1986), *Green Apple on Black Plate*, c. 1921. Oil on canvas, 14 x 12 1/2 inches. Museum purchase with funds from the 1983 Beaux Arts Committee, the Advisory Committee, Mr. and Mrs. Jack McSpadden, and other local donations.

Georgia O'Keeffe's single consuming inspiration was natural forms. She is best known for her landscapes, particularly those of the American Southwest, and for her large canvases of individual flowers. Her paintings combine an accuracy of perceived form, lyrical transformation, and abstraction. Especially in her early work, such as this still life, her paintings were characterized by evenly-colored forms with hard edges, and emphasis on flat rhythmic pattern, and the juxtaposition of high value contrasts. She claimed, "I see no reason why abstract and realistic art can't live side by side. The principles are the same."

A staple of English dessert menus for centuries, creams usually consist of the three basic ingredients—milk or water, sugar, and eggs—with a particular flavoring. They are relatively easy to make and the flavors are as extensive as the imagination. We have included two from *The Modern Art of Cookery* that are long-time English favorites, along with our updated recommendations. We have halved the recipes, but they work well full also.

We have upgraded the Lemon Cream by using cornstarch rather than just eggs to thicken, meaning one egg will suffice. You will find it is much easier and foolproof, and just as delicious as the original. The addition of whipped cream makes it a great dessert on those hot summer days.

❧ A CHOCOLATE CREAM

To a quart of milk [*2 cups half-and-half*] put a quarter of a pound of lump-sugar [*2/3 cup granulated*], and boil them about fifteen minutes [heat to boiling point]; beat up the yolk of an egg, and stir it in; let it have three or four boils, take it off the fire, and put chocolate to it, till it has coloured the cream [*2 squares (2ounces) unsweetened chocolate; shave or grate chocolate and add slowly to cream mixture, stirring over low heat until chocolate is melted*]; set it on the fire, let it boil for a minute or two, and strain it [*not necessary*]: Serve it in china dishes. [*Pour into individual serving dishes and refrigerate for several hours to allow cream to thicken. Delicious served topped with whipped cream.*]

❧ TO MAKE LEMON CREAM

To a pint of water [*1 cup*], add a pound of double refined sugar [*1 cup granulated sugar plus 2 teaspoons cornstarch*], and a piece of lemon-peel; set it on the fire to boil [*boil mixture until it thickens, stirring constantly*], and then let it stand till cold; beat up the whites of six eggs, and one yolk 1 whole egg [*1 whole egg*], with a tea-spoonful of orange flower water, squeeze the juice of four [*2*] lemons, stir all together, and strain it through a fine sieve into the syrup, take out the lemon-peel, and set it over a gentle fire, stirring it one way till it is ready to boil, and taking off the scum as it rises, till it is thick as cream; rest in a good deal of the peel [*stir in grated peel of 1 lemon*], and put it into glasses. You may put into the glasses lemon-peel cut long and very thin. [*We suggest refrigerating the mixture until is is chilled; then just before serving, whip 1 cup of whipping cream and fold it into the chilled mixture. Serve in individual dessert dishes topped with lemon zests.*]

❧ CHOCOLATE AMARETTO MOUSSE

Serves 4 to 6

12 ounces bitter or semi-sweet chocolate
2 eggs
3 tablespoons amaretto liqueur
1 cup whipping cream
2 tablespoons sugar
2 teaspoons vanilla

- Melt chocolate in a large bowl over simmering water or in microwave.
- Remove from heat; beat in egg yolks. Mixture may bind.
- Using an electric mixer, beat in the liqueur until smooth.
- With clean, dry beatters, beat the egg whites with 1 tablespoon sugar till soft peaks form.
- Gently fold whites into chocolate mixture.
- Whip cream with remaining sugar and vanilla until soft peaks form.
- Fold into the chocolate mixture.
- Divide into individual servings, cover, and refrigerate.

❧ TO MAKE ALMOND CHEESCAKES

Blanch half a pound of Jordan almonds [*1 8–ounce can almond paste or 1 cup almonds that have been pulverized in a food processor*], beat them fine with orange flower water [*optional*]; beat up six yolks and two whites of eggs [*1 whole egg, plus 3 yolks*], strain them [*not necessary*] to half a pound of lump sugar sifted [*1 cup granulated*], and a little beaten mace [*optional*]; grate in some lemon peel very fine [*grated rind of 1 lemon*]; melt about half a pound of fresh butter [*1/2 cup*], and mix all very well together; put a puff paste at the bottom of the patty pans [*see p. 78 for pastry recipe*], fill them up, and take care they are not over-baked. [*Bake at 400°. These can be baked as individual tarts using muffin tins or in a 10–inch tart pan. Use 2 12–count muffin tins for the individual tarts. Roll out the pastry 1/4–inch thick and cut in 3–inch circles; place each in a cup and fill 3/4 full with filling. Bake small tarts 15 to 20 minutes; large, single tart 20 to 30 minutes or until top is a light golden brown.*]

This recipe for almond tarts from *The Modern Art of Cookery* is the eighteenth-century version of one used in English kitchens for at least 600 years, and probably longer. Although the original and this version have no cheese, they are the precursors to our own cheesecakes. Known as Maids of Honor or Richmond Maids, in honor of the queen's ladies in waiting, recipes for this dish can be found in cookbooks published as long ago as Richard II's *The Forme of Cury*, c. 1390, and were then known as Daryols. They are, and have been traditionally, served at tea, and are extra delicious when served topped with fresh fruit, particularly berries.

245

❧ SIMPLE CHOCOLATE CHEESECAKE

Serves 8 to 10

1 [8–ounce] package cream cheese, softened
1/2 cup mayonnaise
1/2 cup sugar
2 eggs
6 ounces semi-sweet chocolate, melted
   (white or milk chocolate may also be used)
1 teaspoon vanilla extract
1 tablespoon favorite liqueur: orange liqueur, amaretto, coffee liqueur
1 9–inch graham cracker or chocolate crumb crust

- Beat cream cheese and mayonnaise until blended.
- Add sugar, 1 tablespoon at a time, beating after each addition.
- Add eggs one at a time, and beat well.
- Add chocolate, vanilla, and liqueur.
- Pour into a crumb crust.
- Bake for 35 to 40 minutes at 350°, until knife comes out clean.

❧ DR. DON'S ALMOST-NO-FAT NEW YORK CHEESECAKE

Serves 8

1/4 cup butter or margarine substitute
1 [16–ounce] package cream cheese substitute, such as Healthy Choice or Philly
1 [16–ounce] carton no-fat ricotta cheese
1 1/2 cups sugar
1 carton Egg Beaters [equal to 4 eggs]
3 tablespoons flour
3 tablespoons cornstarch
2 1/2 teaspoons vanilla
1 [16–ounce] carton no-fat sour cream

- Melt butter or margarine substitute and set aside to cool.
- Cream together the cream cheese, ricotta cheese, and sugar.
- Add egg substitute a little at a time, beating well after each addition.
- Add melted butter substitute, flour, cornstarch, and vanilla and mix well.
- Fold in sour cream.
- Pour batter into ungreased 9 or 10–inch springform pan and bake at 325° for
  1 hour. The cake will be soft in the center.
- Turn heat off and do not open oven door. Let stand in oven at least 2 hours.
  Remove from oven, cool, and refrigerate for 2 more hours before serving.

This recipe comes from our curator of Asian Art, Dr. Donald Wood. Along with being an expert in the field of Asian art, he is also our resident expert on cheesecakes. A terrific chef, Don is also conscious of healthy, low-fat eating and claims this version of New York cheesecake is so close to the original you can't tell the difference. He has also contributed the sinfully delicious Chocolate Amaretto Mousse on page 245.

246

❧ CHEESECAKE WITH CRANBERRY TOPPING

Serves 8

Crust

1 1/2 cups graham-cracker crumbs

1/4 cup sugar

1/4 cup chopped almonds

1/4 cup melted butter

1/4 teaspoon salt

Filling

2 [12–ounce] cartoons cottage cheese

1 cup sugar

4 eggs

1 teaspoon vanilla

Topping

2 cups sour cream

1 tablespoon sugar

1 teaspoon vanilla

Cranberry topping

1/2 cup sugar

1 tablespoon cornstarch

1 [16–ounce] can whole cranberry sauce

1/4 cup orange juice

2 tablespoons grated orange rind

247

- Mix graham-cracker crumbs, sugar, almonds, and salt together, and mix in melted butter.
- Line a 9–inch springform pan with the mixture.
- In a blender or with a mixer, blend the cottage cheese until it is smooth.
- Add the sugar and mix.
- Beat the eggs in one at a time; stir in the vanilla.
- Pour into the crust and bake at 375° for 40 minutes.
- Mix sour cream, 1 tablespoon sugar, and 1 teaspoon vanilla together and spread on the top of the cheesecake; bake an additional 5 minutes at 475°.
- Drain the canned cranberries through a strainer and add enough water to the liquid to make 3/4 cup.
- Mix the liquid, sugar, cornstarch, and orange juice in a saucepan.
- Heat, stirring, until it comes to a boil. Reduce heat and simmer for 5 minutes.
- Remove from heat and add berries and orange rind.
- Cool for 5 minutes and spread on the cooled cheesecake.

❧ AMARETTO CHEESECAKE

Serves 12

1 1/2 cups graham cracker crumbs
2 tablespoons sugar
1 teaspoon ground cinnamon
1/4 cup plus 2 tablespoons butter, melted
3 [8–ounce] packages cream cheese, softened
1 cup sugar
4 eggs
1 [8–ounce] carton sour cream
1 tablespoon plus 1 teaspoon sugar
1 tablespoon amaretto
1/4 cup toasted sliced almonds
1 [1.2–ounce] chocolate candy bar, grated

- Combine graham cracker crumbs, 2 tablespoons sugar, cinnamon, and butter; mix well.
- Firmly press mixture into bottom and 1/2–inch up the sides of a 9–inch springform pan.
- Beat cream cheese with electric mixer until light and fluffy. Gradually add 1 cup sugar, mixing well.
- Add eggs, one at a time, beating well after each addition.
- Stir in 1/3 cup amaretto; pour into prepared pan.
- Bake at 375° for 45 to 50 minutes or until set.
- Combine sour cream, 1 tablespoon plus 1 teaspoon sugar, and 1 tablespoon amaretto; stir well, and spoon over the cheesecake.
- Bake at 500° for 5 minutes.
- Let cool to room temperature; then refrigerate 24 to 48 hours. (Cheesecake is best when thoroughly chilled and flavors have time to ripen.)

Garnish with almonds and grated chocolate.

∽ CHOCOLATE CRINKLES

Makes 2 dozen

1/4 cup butter
2 squares unsweetened chocolate
1 cup sugar
2 eggs
1 teaspoon vanilla
1 cup all-purpose flour
Sifted powdered sugar

- Melt butter and chocolate together, and cool briefly.
- Beat in sugar, and then eggs.
- Stir in vanilla.
- Sift flour and baking powder together; add to mixture. Stir.
- Chill at least 30 minutes.
- Roll dough into 1–inch balls.
- Roll in powdered sugar.
- Bake at 375° for 4 to 5 minutes. Do not overcook; cookies will be soft.

∽ MRS. BUGBEE'S GINGER COOKIES

Makes 3 dozen

3/4 cup margarine
1 cup sugar
1/4 cup molasses
1 egg
2 1/2 cups all-purpose flour
1/4 teaspoon salt
1 teaspoon cinnamon
1 tablespoon ginger
1 teaspoon baking powder
2 teaspoons baking soda

- Beat margarine and sugar together until they are creamy.
- Stir in egg and molasses.
- Add dry ingredients and mix well.
- Roll into 1–inch balls, then roll balls in granulated sugar.
- Bake at 350° for 12 to 15 minutes.
- Cool on the cookie sheet for easier removal.

249

Nancy McCormack, exhibition tour coordinator, is the museum's cookie connoisseur, and we have included two of her cookie recipes. She says people always think the flour measurement in this recipe is a mistake; she and the committee assure us it is correct. Nancy also recommends using greased foil to bake these.

∿ LACY OATMEAL COOKIES

Makes 3 dozen

1/2 cup margarine
1 1/2 cups uncooked oats
1/2 cup sugar
1/4 cup brown sugar
1 teaspoon baking powder
1 teaspoon all-purpose flour
1 teaspoon vanilla
1 egg
1/2 cup chopped nuts (optional)

- Melt margarine and pour over oats.
- Blend in sugars, baking powder, and flour.
- Mix in vanilla, egg, and nuts.
- Drop half-teaspoonfuls of dough 2 inches apart on greased cookie sheets.
- Bake for 11 minutes at 325°.
- Let the cookies COOL COMPLETELY before removing them from the cookie sheets.

∿ QUEET'S MELTING MOMENTS

Makes approximately 5 dozen cookies

1 cup butter
3/4 cup sugar
1 1/2 cups all-purpose flour
1/2 teaspoon baking powder
1/2 teaspoon white vinegar
1/2 teaspoon almond extract
Slivered almonds

- Blend butter and sugar together until they are creamy.
- Sift in flour, baking powder, and sugar; mix well.
- Stir in vinegar and almond extract.
- Drop by scant teaspoonfuls onto a greased baking sheet. Press an almond on top of each cookie.
- Bake at 300° for 18 to 20 minutes.

∾ POLISH LEMON BUTTER COOKIES

Makes 2 to 3 dozen

1 cup butter
3/4 cup sugar
5 hard-cooked egg yolks, mashed
Grated rind of one large lemon
Scant teaspoon lemon extract
1 tablespoon sour cream
Just over 2 cups sifted all-purpose flour

- Blend butter and sugar together until creamy; add egg yolks, lemon rind, and lemon extract and mix until well blended.
- Stir in flour. Dough will be soft, but should be easy to work after it has chilled.
- Chill dough overnight so it is firm enough to roll.
- Lightly grease cookie sheets.
- On a lightly floured surface, roll dough 1/4–inch thick. Cut with small cookie cutters. Traditional shapes are six-pointed stars, hearts, diamonds, rectangles, or crescent moons.
- Place on lightly greased cookie sheets, 1 inch apart, and sprinkle with mixture of sugar and cinnamon.
  Or make a mixture of 1 beaten egg and 1 teaspoon milk. Brush this on the cookies and then sprinkle with crushed nuts, poppy seeds, or cinnamon-sugar.
- Bake at 350° for approximately 10 minutes. Do not brown.

Cookies can also be rolled into balls the size of walnuts, then flattened with the bottom of a glass.

This Shortbread recipe is Nancy MaCormack's second cookie recipe and has an interesting story behind it. All shortbreads tasted pretty similar to Nancy until she bought some cookies imported from a remote Scottish locale. They tasted scrumtious, but there was something about them she could not duplicate in her own shortbread cookies, a secret ingredient. She kept reading the ingredient list on the package, and trying various measurements and brands of these to no avail. One day it hit like a bolt out of the blue; the secret ingredient was brown sugar, listed just as sugar on the bag. She tried it and they were a perfect match.

We close the cookie section with two simple cookie recipes from *The Modern Art of Cookery*. The first is for the eighteenth-century version of Scottish Shortbread. Again it is possible to see how delicious, traditional recipes have changed very little over the years. We have cut the amounts in half, but if you need gargantuan numbers of cookies, you can use the full measurements.

Our last cookie recipe, from *The Modern Art of Cookery*, is for what the English normally call biscuits. They are served at tea, are normally dry rather then moist, and frequently include currants or other fruits, or seeds, such as caraway seeds. This recipe is the eighteenth-century English idea of what a French biscuit was like.

❧ SHORTBREAD COOKIES

Makes 2 dozen cookies

1 cup margarine
1/2 cup sifted powdered sugar
1/4 cup light brown sugar
2 cups all-purpose flour
Powdered sugar

- Work sugars and margarine together in a large bowl.
- Add flour in 1/2 cup measures until all ingredients are well blended.
- Sprinkle board with powdered sugar, and knead dough several times.
- Roll out to 1/2–inch thickness. Cut with a cookie cutter, or cut into 2–inch squares.
- Place on baking sheets and refrigerate for 20 minutes.
- Bake at 325° for 15 to 20 minutes.

❧ TO MAKE LITTLE CAKES

To a pound of flour [*4 cups*] add half a pound [*1 cup granulated*] of sugar sifted, half a pound of butter [*1 cup*] well beat, and a little orange-flower water [*optional*]; mix all well together, make them into little cakes, and bake them up on tins. [*Roll out dough 1/4–inch thick and cut into desired shapes. Bake at 350° for 15 to 20 minutes, until the bottoms just begin to brown.*]

❧ TO MAKE BISCUITS THE FRENCH WAY

Weigh four eggs [*3 large eggs*], and add the same weight of fine flour, and sugar pounded [*1 1/2 cups flour and 3/4 cup granulated sugar*]; beat the whites of the eggs to a froth, and the yolks by themselves [*use an electric mixer or wire whisk*]; put in half an ounce [*1 tablespoon*] of candied lemon-peel cut very fine, then by degrees put in the flour and sugar; put the yolks in last, with a clean spoon; mix all very well together; shape them with a spoon on writing paper, and sift pounded sugar over them [*dough will be soft; drop by spoonfuls and spread into circles with the back of the spoon and sprinkle with sugar*]; bake them in an oven not too hot, and when they are taken out, loosen them from the paper, while they are warm, with a knife. When they are cold, put them by for use. [*Bake at 350° for 10 to 15 minutes, but do not let them brown. Use a non-stick baking sheet or use parchment or wax paper to bake them on; remove them immediately from the baking sheet or they will stick. They can be stored in a cookie tin.*]

❧ KLINGLER'S RUM-RAISIN BALLS

Makes 20 to 24 balls

3/4 cups raisins, chopped
3 tablespoons dark rum
10 ounces semisweet chocolate
1/2 cup butter
1 cup powdered sugar
Chocolate sprinkles

- Soak raisins in rum for 1 hour.
- Heat chocolate in the top of a double boiler until it is soft, but not hot. Remove from heat.
- Blend in butter, then powdered sugar.
- Stir in raisins and rum.
- If mixture is too soft to work with, refrigerate until it is workable.
- Form into balls the size of walnuts and roll in chocolate sprinkles to cover.

Our last restaurant recipe is for a holiday favorite and comes from Klingler's European Bakery located in Vestavia Hills. They have been at this location for only several years, but already have a reputation for some of the finest European-type baked goods and catering services in the area. We hope you enjoy their recipe for this classic candy.

❧ ORANGE CANDY

Makes approximately 24 pieces

2 cups sugar
1/2 cup light corn syrup
1/2 cup whipping cream
1/4 cup butter or margarine
1/4 teaspoon salt
Peel from 1 orange, cut in thin slivers
1 cup pecans

- In a medium-sized, heavy saucepan, mix sugar, corn syrup, unwhipped cream, and butter or margarine together. Add orange peel.
- Cook over medium heat until mixture forms a soft ball when dropped in cold water, or when candy thermometer registers 234° to 240°.
- Remove pan from the heat and add nuts. Let stand 10 minutes.
- Beat mixture until thick. Drop by teaspoonfuls onto wax paper.

The Altlanta matron who created this candy recipe kept it a carefully guarded secret for many years. Until her death, she presented the candy as a Christmas gift each year to her special friends. After her death, however, the secret came out, and was passed on to Helen Smith who now shares it with us.

253

Albert Bierstadt (American, 1820–1902), *Looking Down Yosemite Valley, California,* 1865. Oil on canvas, 60 x 84 inches. Gift of the Birmingham Public Library.

The second half of the nineteenth century was the age of discovery of the American West. A number of geological and geographical surveys were sponsored by the federal government to chart and record nature's majesty and wonder in this pristine and natural environment. These expeditions often included artists and photographers to visually record nature's phenomena. Along with accompanying two of these expeditions, Bierstadt also traveled to the West on his own, recording what he saw in hundreds of sketches and watercolors. Back in his studio, he transformed these studies into magnificent canvases done in the romantic spirit of the time. *Looking Down Yosemite Valley, California* ranks as one of the finest landscapes of the American West.

❧ OLD SPARKES FAMILY PRALINES

Makes about 18 candies

2 cups firmly packed brown sugar
1/2 cup whipping cream
1/4 teaspoon salt
1 cup pecan halves
2 tablespoons butter or margarine
1 teaspoon vanilla

- Lightly butter a long sheet of aluminum foil.
- In a large saucepan, combine sugar, cream, and salt. Bring to a full boil, stirring constantly. Reduce heat to medium-low and begin timing. Keep candy at a low boil for 3 minutes.
- Without removing it from heat, add pecans and butter or margarine. When mixture returns to a full boil, begin timing again. Keep at a low boil for 2 minutes, stirring constantly (or until a drop of the mixture forms a firm ball in a cup of cool water, 242° to 248° on a candy thermometer).
- Remove candy from heat and let cool for 3 to 5 minutes.
- Add vanilla. Beat mixture with a wooden spoon for 2 minutes, or until candy is clinging to the nuts but still glossy.
- Drop by spoonfuls onto buttered foil. Cool candy completely before removing from foil.

❧ TO MAKE A WHIPT SYLLABUB

Take a quart of cream not too thick [*4 cups cream*], a pint of sack [*2 cups sherry*], and the juice of two lemons, sweeten it to your palate, and whisk it up very well; take it off with a spoon, and put it into glasses. They must not be made long before they are used.

We close our book with a most appropriate recipe from *The Modern Art of Cookery*. The ties between England and the American South go back generations to when the English settlers came here and stayed, many in what is now Alabama.

The syllabub is a traditional Southern drink for festive occasions, and finds its roots in English cooking, as attested to by this recipe. It is another of many English/American South recipes that is almost exactly the same today as it was 300 years ago. It is between a dessert and a drink, and "must not be made long before they are used."

255

Contemporary recipes are shown in regular type, old recipes in italics.

INDEX OF ARTWORK

262

263

265

267

Please use the order form at the right to order more copies of *Culinary Masterpieces from the Birmingham Museum of Art*

Send to:
Culinary Masterpieces
Birmingham Museum of Art
2000 Eighth Avenue North
Birmingham, Alabama 35203-2278

Proceeds from the sale of this cookbook benefit the Birmingham Museum of Art

---

Culinary Masterpieces

Birmingham Museum of Art, 2000 Eighth Avenue North, Birmingham, Alabama 35203-2278

Please send _____ copies of *Culinary Masterpieces* at $19.95 each plus $3.00 each shipping and handling ($22.95 per copy ordered)

Enclosed is a check for $_____, payable to: Birmingham Museum of Art.

I prefer to pay by credit card: _____ VISA _____ Mastercard
    Account number _____ Expiration date _____
    Cardholder's signature _____

Send to:
Name _____
Address _____
City_____ State _____ Zip _____

Culinary Masterpieces

Birmingham Museum of Art, 2000 Eighth Avenue North, Birmingham, Alabama 35203-2278

Please send _____ copies of *Culinary Masterpieces* at $19.95 each plus $3.00 each shipping and handling ($22.95 per copy ordered)

Enclosed is a check for $_____, payable to: Birmingham Museum of Art.

I prefer to pay by credit card: _____ VISA _____ Mastercard
    Account number _____ Expiration date _____
    Cardholder's signature _____

Send to:
Name _____
Address _____
City_____ State _____ Zip _____

Culinary Masterpieces

Birmingham Museum of Art, 2000 Eighth Avenue North, Birmingham, Alabama 35203-2278

Please send _____ copies of *Culinary Masterpieces* at $19.95 each plus $3.00 each shipping and handling ($22.95 per copy ordered)

Enclosed is a check for $_____, payable to: Birmingham Museum of Art.

I prefer to pay by credit card: _____ VISA _____ Mastercard
    Account number _____ Expiration date _____
    Cardholder's signature _____

Send to:
Name _____
Address _____
City_____ State _____ Zip _____